GEORGE ELIOT AND HER READERS

A Selection of Contemporary Reviews

GEORGE ELIOT
and her readers

A Selection of
Contemporary Reviews

Editors
JOHN HOLMSTROM
and
LAURENCE LERNER
with a linking commentary by
LAURENCE LERNER

THE BODLEY HEAD

LONDON

Acknowledgements are due to the following for permission to reproduce material used in this book:

William Blackwood and Sons Ltd
The Contemporary Review
The Daily Telegraph
John Farquharson Ltd
London Electrotype Agency
The New Statesman
The Observer
The Spectator
The Times
Yale University Press

© Laurence Lerner and John Holmstrom, 1966
Printed and bound in Great Britain for
The Bodley Head Ltd
9 Bow Street, London, wc2
by William Clowes & Sons Ltd, Beccles
Set in Monotype Scotch Roman No. 1
First published 1966

CONTENTS

Preface

This anthology of criticism is intended to show what contemporaries thought of the novels of George Eliot. The world is full, nowadays, of critical anthologies which offer us a range of interpretations of the great writers of the past, by the great critics of the present; such books serve many functions, but the one thing they do not tell us, in their wealth of subtle, profound and ingenious commentary, is what impression the writers made on the readers for whom they were, in the first place, writing. George Eliot may, in a sense, have been writing for Lionel Trilling and William Empson all the time; but, in another and more obvious sense, she was writing for the eight thousand readers who bought *Adam Bede*, and the dozen or two critics who reviewed it. Those are the people here represented.

This volume tells of two things: of the novels, and of the impression they made. It therefore has a double interest. It has the interest of all literary criticism, illuminating the books discussed, relating them to the critic's own experience of life; and a historical interest, showing us what the Victorians looked for in their favourite novelists. As far as the first (critical) interest is concerned, some of the critics are obviously worth more than others. Few reviewers are as penetrating as Sidney Colvin was on George Eliot (or Edmund Gosse on Hardy), and some of those included—but not many—are quite worthless. These latter are here for their historical interest, for our picture of the Victorian response is incomplete if it includes only the intelligent critics. Yet in another, and perhaps more genuine, sense of 'historical', a true historical reconstruction ought to pay particular attention to the best: Colvin speaks more truly for what readers were really thinking—or groping towards thinking—in the 1870s than do most of the everyday reviewers. These two approaches, critical and historical, are easily distinguished in theory, but almost impossible to disentangle in practice. Few readers of this volume will be interested in one without any touch of the other; and it goes without saying that even the most

9

historically minded reader will get little from the critics if he has never read the novelist.

If all the novels had been given equal treatment, we would either have had to sacrifice full treatment of any, or else make the volume impossibly long. We have therefore selected three for really thorough coverage, but have included at least one notice of each of the others. Choosing the three was not easy: we settled on *The Mill on the Floss*, the finest of her early novels; *Middlemarch*, her masterpiece; and *Daniel Deronda*, not only because one half of it is the equal of anything she ever wrote, but also because the other—the Jewish—half drew such an interesting response. It was tempting to add the underrated *Felix Holt* as a fourth—but then we would have been tempted to add a fifth, and a sixth.

The main source of material has been the daily, weekly and quarterly papers published in England, and these we have combed as thoroughly as we could. When we found interesting material elsewhere, we have included it. Each section contains a short note on the publishing history of the novel; then the reviews; then an editorial commentary. The general section at the end is taken both from articles on George Eliot's work as a whole, and also from generalising digressions in the reviews. Divergences from modern usage in the spelling, punctuation and syntax of the material have been retained, but mere errors have been corrected. The authors of unsigned reviews, when we have been able to identify these, are named in square brackets. Some of this information has come through the kindness of editors and librarians of journals: Mr G. D. Blackwood of William Blackwood and Sons; Mr Jeremy Potter, of the *New Statesman;* Mr Charles Seaton of *The Spectator*. Mr Adrian Peasgood, of the University of Sussex Library, has been very helpful. Our greatest helper has helped unwittingly: Gordon Haight's edition of *The George Eliot Letters* is a masterpiece of scholarship which has saved us enormous trouble, and added to the value of our book.

JOHN HOLMSTROM
LAURENCE LERNER

Biographical Note

Marian Evans was born on 22 November 1819 at South Farm, Arbury, Warwickshire. She grew up in the country and (later) at Coventry, where she replaced her early evangelicalism with the 'advanced' opinions she absorbed from her friends, the Brays and the Hennells. Her earliest literary work was her translation of Strauss and Feuerbach, the German humanist critics of Christtianity; her version of Strauss's *Life of Jesus* was published in 1846, that of Feuerbach's *Essence of Christianity* in 1854. She was assistant editor of *The Westminster Review* from 1851 to 1854. In 1854 she began living with G. H. Lewes, whom she could not marry because he had a wife living whom he was unable to divorce. She began writing fiction at the age of thirty-six. The rest of her life was outwardly uneventful: increasing fame, frequent travel on the continent, friendships with most of the interesting figures of the time, intense inner uncertainty and a happy marriage. Lewes died in 1878, and about two years later she married J. W. Cross, an old friend very much younger than herself. She died in December 1880, seven months after her marriage to Cross.

Her books, with dates of first publication in book form:

1858   *Scenes of Clerical Life*
1859   *Adam Bede*
1860   *The Mill on the Floss*
1861   *Silas Marner*
1863   *Romola*
1866   *Felix Holt*
1868   *The Spanish Gypsy* (dramatic poem)
1872   *Middlemarch*
1874   *Jubal and Other Poems*
1876   *Daniel Deronda*
1879   *Impressions of Theophrastus Such* (essays)

I · SCENES OF CLERICAL LIFE

G.E.'s *Journal*, September 1856

September 1856 made a new era in my life, for it was then I began to write fiction. It had always been a vague dream of mine that some time or other I might write a novel; and my shadowy conception of what the novel was to be, varied, of course, from one epoch of my life to another. But I never went further towards the actual writing of the novel than an introductory chapter describing a Staffordshire village and the life of the neighbouring farm-houses; and as the years passed on I lost any hope that I should ever be able to write a novel, just as I desponded about everything else in my future life. I always thought I was deficient in dramatic power, both of construction and dialogue, but I felt I should be at my ease in the descriptive parts of a novel. My 'introductory chapter' was pure description, though there were good materials in it for dramatic presentation. It happened to be among the papers I had with me in Germany, and one evening at Berlin something led me to read it to George. He was struck with it as a bit of concrete description, and it suggested to him the possibility of my being able to write a novel, though he distrusted—indeed disbelieved in—my possession of any dramatic power. Still, he began to think that I might as well try some time what I could do in fiction; and by-and-by, when we came back to England, and I had greater success than he ever expected in other kinds of writing, his impression that it was worth while to see how far my mental power would go, towards the production of a novel, was strengthened. He began to say very positively, 'You must try and write a story,' and when we were at Tenby he urged me to begin at once. I deferred it, however, after my usual fashion, with work that does not present itself as an absolute duty. But one morning as I was lying in bed thinking what should be the subject of my first story, my thoughts merged themselves into a dreamy doze, and I imagined

myself writing a story, of which the title was 'The Sad Fortunes
of the Reverend Amos Barton.' I was soon wide awake again and
told G. He said, 'Oh, what a capital title!' and from that time I
had settled in my mind that this should be my first story. George
used to say, 'It may be a failure—it may be that you are unable to
write fiction. Or perhaps it may be just good enough to warrant
you trying again.' Again, 'You may write a *chef-d'oeuvre* at once—
there's no telling.' But his prevalent impression was, that though
I could hardly write a *poor* novel, my effort would want the highest
quality of fiction—dramatic presentation. He used to say, 'You
have wit, description, and philosophy—those go a good way towards
the production of a novel. It is worth while for you to try the
experiment.'

We determined that if my story turned out good enough, we
would send it to Blackwood; but G. thought the more probable
result was that I should have to lay it aside and try again.

But when we returned to Richmond, I had to write my article
on 'Silly Novels', and my review of Contemporary Literature for
the 'Westminster', so that I did not begin my story till September
22. After I had begun it, as we were walking in the park, I mentioned to G. that I had thought of the plan of writing a series of
stories, containing sketches drawn from my own observation of the
clergy, and calling them 'Scenes from Clerical Life,' opening with
'Amos Barton.' He at once accepted the notion as a good one—
fresh and striking; and about a week afterwards, when I read him
the first part of 'Amos,' he had no longer any doubt about my
ability to carry out the plan. The scene at Cross Farm, he said,
satisfied him that I had the very element he had been doubtful
about—it was clear I could write good dialogue. There still
remained the question whether I could command any pathos; and
that was to be decided by the mode in which I treated Milly's
death. One night G. went to town on purpose to leave me a quiet
evening for writing it. I wrote the chapter from the news brought
by the shepherd to Mrs Hackit, to the moment when Amos is
dragged from the bedside, and I read it to G. when he came home.
We both cried over it, and then he came up to me and kissed me,
saying, 'I think your pathos is better than your fun.'

❡'Amos Barton' was published in *Blackwood's Magazine*, to
which Lewes was already a contributor. It was followed by two

other stories, 'Mr Gilfil's Love Story' and 'Janet's Repentance', and the three were published as a volume under the title *Scenes of Clerical Life*.

G.E.'s *Journal*, 2 January 1858

George has returned this evening from a week's visit to Vernon Hill. On coming up-stairs he said—'I have some very pretty news for you,—something in my pocket.' I was at a loss to conjecture, and thought confusedly of possible opinions from admiring readers, when he drew the 'Times' from his pocket—to-day's number, containing a review of the 'Scenes of Clerical Life.' He had happened to ask a gentleman in the railway carriage coming up to London to allow him to look at the 'Times,' and felt quite agitated and tremulous when his eyes alighted on the review. Finding he had time to go into town before the train started, he bought a copy there. It is a highly favourable notice, and, as far as it goes, appreciatory.

The Times, 2 January 1858

Of the other recent fictions we have been most impressed with the series of *Scenes from Clerical Life*, which have been just reprinted from *Blackwood's Magazine*, and which are now claimed by Mr. George Eliot—a name unknown to us. It is quite possible that this may be a mere *nom de plume*, and we are not curious to inquire at all upon this point. But we should be greatly surprised to hear that the real writer was previously known under any other appellation, for, like others who have speculated on his identity while these tales were publishing, we cannot assign his peculiarities to any living novelist. Were these the early days of Galt or Lockhart, or could even Crabbe come back from the grave in a softer mood and with a resolve to discard versification for prose, we should have some basis for conjecture; but now we have none. We lay no particular stress on the parochial limits of the scene and the parochial relations of its occupants. We observe only that the sources of interest are chiefly domestic and homely, and that there is a careful study of familiar types, and an absence of exaggeration in their treatment which recall the productions of a school of fiction akin to that of Wilkie in pictorial art. A sobriety which is shown to be compatible with strength, clear and simple descriptions, and a combination of humour with pathos in depicting ordinary situations, are characteristics of this school, and are evinced by Mr. Eliot.

Of the three stories comprised in these clerical scenes, we prefer the 'Rev. Mr. Gilfil's Love Story' to 'the Sad Fortunes of the Rev. Amos Barton,' or to 'Janet's Repentance.' It has the peculiarity of being a retrospect commencing from Mr. Gilfil's death, and we are drawn into it from an intimation of what the hero became in the decline of life, when his wound was cicatrized, and love had given place to softened regret. The picture of Mr. Gilfil at this latter stage is charmingly painted with firm and effective touches, and, as Sir Walter Scott said of the Wakefield Vicar, though each touch serves to show that he is made of mortal mould and is full of human frailties, the effect of the whole is to reconcile us to human nature. The charm, too, is sustained by an adherence to probability and by the allowance for influences which the incidents alone do not involve, but which we know to make up a large proportion of every man's life. The artificial elements of the story are thus kept within bounds, the tendency to sacrifice to their exigencies is compensated by a reference to the actual results of experience, and a closer resemblance than usual is thus established between the conceptions of fiction and the realities of the world. . . .   [SAMUEL LUCAS]

❡ G.E. had copies of the *Scenes* sent to writers she admired. By far the most interesting letter she received was a very shrewd one from Dickens:

TAVISTOCK HOUSE, LONDON,
Monday, 17*th Jan.* 1858
MY DEAR SIR,—I have been so strongly affected by the two first tales in the book you have had the kindness to send me, through Messrs Blackwood, that I hope you will excuse my writing to you to express my admiration of their extraordinary merit. The exquisite truth and delicacy, both of the humour and the pathos of these stories, I have never seen the like of; and they have impressed me in a manner that I should find it very difficult to describe to you, if I had the impertinence to try.

In addressing these few words of thankfulness to the creator of the Sad Fortunes of the Rev. Amos Barton, and the sad love-story of Mr Gilfil, I am (I presume) bound to adopt the name that it pleases that excellent writer to assume. I can suggest no better one: but I should have been strongly disposed, if I had been left to my own devices, to address the said writer as a woman. I have observed what seemed to me such womanly touches in those moving fictions, that the assurance on the title-page is insufficient to satisfy me even now. If they originated with no woman, I believe that no man ever before had the art of making himself mentally so like a woman since the world began.

You will not suppose that I have any vulgar wish to fathom your secret. I mention the point as one of great interest to me—not of mere curiosity. If it should ever suit your convenience and inclination to show me the face of the man, or woman, who has written so charmingly, it will be a very memorable occasion to me. If otherwise, I shall always hold that impalpable personage in loving attachment and respect, and shall yield myself up to all future utterances from the same source, with a perfect confidence in their making me wiser and better.—Your obliged and faithful servant and admirer, [CHARLES DICKENS] GEORGE ELIOT, Esq.

George Eliot had already met Dickens when she received this letter: he had taken the chair at a meeting of authors in Chapman's house in the Strand in 1852. She wrote to her friends the Brays that he filled the chair remarkably well, but that his appearance was disappointing: 'no benevolence in the face, and, I think, little in the head,—the anterior lobe not by any means remarkable.'

When Dickens learned who she was he wrote to her again, praising *Adam Bede*, and saying, 'You must not suppose that I am writing this to *you*. I have been saying it over and over again, here and elsewhere, until I feel in a ludicrously apologetic state for repeating myself on this paper' (10 July 1859). Soon after that they met, and their friendship continued, though they were never intimate. 'He is a man one can thoroughly enjoy talking to,' she wrote to Sara Hennell on 11 November 1859, '—there is a strain of real seriousness along with his keenness and humour.' After his death, however, she remarked that his latter years wore 'a melancholy aspect . . .—the feverish pursuit of loud effects and money'.

II · ADAM BEDE

❧ This was George Eliot's first full-length novel: written during 1857–8, and published by Blackwood's on 1 February 1859. We give the bulk of *The Times* review, and one or two other representative extracts.

The Times, 12 April 1859

There can be no mistake about *Adam Bede*. It is a first-rate novel, and its author takes rank at once among the masters of the art. Hitherto known but as the writer of certain tales to which he gave the modest title of 'Scenes,' and which displayed only the buds of what we have here in full blossom, he has produced a work which, after making every allowance for certain crudities of execution, impresses us with a sense of the novelist's maturity of thought and feeling. Very seldom are so much freshness of style and warmth of emotion seen combined with so much solid sense and ripened observation. We have a pleasant feeling of security in either laughing or crying with such a companion. Our laughter shall not be trifling, and our tears shall not be maudlin. We need not fear to yield ourselves entirely to all the enchantments of the wizard whose first article of belief is the truism which very few of us comprehend until it has been knocked into us by years of experience—that we are all alike—that the human heart is one. All the novelists and all the dramatists that have ever lived have set themselves to exhibit the differences between man and man. Here, they seem to say, are circumstances precisely similar, and yet mark how various are the characters which grow out of these circumstances. The Pharisee in the Temple felt that he was different from other men, thanking his God for it; and which of us, in the immaturity of experience, is not forced chiefly to consider the differences between ourselves and other men, often utterly forgetting the grand fact of an underlying unity? Here we see monsters, and there we see angels, alien faces and inaccessible natures. It is only

2

after much beating about, long intercourse with society, and many strange discoveries and detections, that the truism which we never doubted becomes a great reality to us, and we feel that man is like to man even as face answers to face in a glass. It is in the enunciation of this difficult truism that Mr. Thackeray differs from all previous novelists. It is the supreme motive of all that he has written, and the key to all the criticism that has been poured upon him. There is not a page of his works in which we do not hear the author exclaiming, 'You see all these people that appear to be so different; I tell you they are all alike. You despise that wretch;—thou art the man. See what a monster I have painted;—I am that monster. Good friends, let us all shake hands; external differences are very well and very amusing, but I beseech of you to think less of the external differences than of the prevailing identity. We shall have less of laughing at each other and tearing each other to pieces when we come to recognize that there is no inherent distinction between Tyburn Jack and the Lord Mayor, between Sally, the cook, who looks after the dripping and thinks tenderly of the policeman, and the great lady intent upon pin-money and wondering whether Arthur is going to offer his arm to the supper-room. People are bad, no doubt, but they are no worse than we are; we think kindly of ourselves—we give fine names to our own faults, we find excuses for our errors. Pray let us give the fine names all round; let us think kindly of others; let us excuse our neighbours; let us not condemn the world wholesale.' With regard to which philosophy two things are to be noted,—the first that, whether true or false, it is the reverse of uncharitable; it is the expression of a warm human sympathy. In point of fact, it is but a secular rendering of the deepest sentiment of Christianity—the sense of personal unworthiness in the presence of God, which teaches us the weakness of our nature and how near the very best of us are of kin to the chief of sinners and the most degraded of beings. The second, that a novelist, writing in accordance with this philosophy, has a most difficult task to perform. It is comparatively easy to draw a character so long as we dwell mainly on points of difference and contrast. But when the object is to touch lightly on mere peculiarities, and to dwell mainly on those traits which we have all in common, and, which, therefore, are anything but salient, the difficulty of the task is enormously increased.

We do not mean for one moment to detract from Mr. George Elliot's originality when we say that after his own fashion he follows this difficult path in which Mr. Thackeray leads the way. He has fully reached that idea which it is so easy to confess in words, but so hard to admit into the secret heart, that we are all alike, that our natures are the same, and that there is not the mighty difference which is usually assumed between high and low, rich and poor, the fool and the sage, the best of us and the worst of us. In general, it is only matured minds that reach this state of feeling—minds that have gone through a good deal and seen through a good deal; and our author has precisely this broad sympathy and large tolerance, combined with ripe reflection and finished style, which we admire in Mr. Thackeray. Here the comparison ends. Mr. Elliot differs so widely from Mr. Thackeray in his mode of working out the philosophy which is common to both that some of our readers may wonder how we could ever see a resemblance between him and the great painter of human vanities and weakness. Whereas Mr. Thackeray is, to the great disgust of many young ladies, continually asserting that we have all got an evil corner in our hearts, and little deceitful ways of working, Mr. Elliot is good enough to tell us that we have all a remnant of Eden in us, that people are not so bad as is commonly supposed, and that every one has affectionate fibres in his nature—fine, loveable traits, in his character. The novel before us is crowded with characters, but they are loveable. It is true that one individual is guilty of seduction, that another is guilty of murder, and that a third is a greedy old miser, but the author finds good in them all and lets them off easy, not only with pardon, but in the two former cases loaded with affectionate sympathy. If in this way he has gone to an extreme, it is a fault which most persons will readily forgive, since it enables them to think better of poor fallen human nature. How kindly he excuses that selfish old Squire who has not a thought for one human being apparently! 'I believe,' says his grandson and heir, 'if I were to break my neck he would feel it the greatest misfortune that could befall him, and yet it seems a pleasure to him to make my life a series of petty annoyances.' Then says the parson, with his kindly philosophy, and with a phrase which puts a fine gloss on all manner of selfishness, 'Ah, my boy, it is not only woman's love that is ἀπέρωτος ἔρως, as old Æschylus calls it. There's plenty of "unloving love" in the world of a masculine kind.' The ingenuity with which the kindhearted Squire is thus made to fit into a new and improved edition of human nature, gilt-edged, is characteristic. Mr. Thackeray, on the contrary, would have made us unwilling to condemn the man by showing us that we, too, have our selfish fits, and that especially the grandson who makes the complaint is longing for the death of the useless old Fogie. But, although tending to such opposite results, the principle upon which both novelists work is the same. Here is a sentence which Thackeray himself might have written:—'Before you despise Adam as deficient in penetration, pray ask yourself if you were ever predisposed to believe evil of any pretty woman—if you ever could, without hard headbreaking demonstration, believe evil of the one supremely pretty woman who has bewitched you. No; people who love downy peaches are apt not to think of the stone, and sometimes jar their teeth terribly against it.' We might quote a long passage to a similar effect from the first chapter of the second volume, but it will be sufficient to give one sentence in which the author represents human affection as triumphing over every obstacle of mental deficiency and personal appearance. After mentioning the ugly fellows with squat figures, ill-shapen nostrils, and dingy complexions, whose miniatures are kissed in secret by motherly lips, he says:—'And I believe there have been plenty of young heroes, of middle stature and feeble beards, who have felt quite sure they could never love anything more insignificant than a Diana, and yet have found themselves in middle life happily settled with a wife who waddles.'. . .

It will be evident that in order to establish the identity of man with man an author must travel a good deal into the region of latent thoughts, and unconscious or but semi-conscious feelings. There is infinite variety in what we express; there is a wonderful monotony in that great world of life which never comes into the light, but moves within us like the beating of the heart and the breathing of the lungs—a constant, though unobserved influence. It is in this twilight of the human soul that our novelist most delights to make his observations. Old Lisbeth Bede says of her son Adam, who is continually visiting the Poysers with the object (unknown even to himself) of seeing Dinah Morris:—'Eh, donna tell me what thee't sure on; thee know'st nought about it. What's he allays going to the Poysers' for, if he didna want t' see her? He goes twice where he used t' go once. Happen he knows na as he wants t' see her; *he knows na as I put salt in's broth, but he'd miss it pretty quick if it warna there.*' It is to the world of thoughts indicated in Mrs. Bede's very homely remark that the author has turned his chief attention. Like Mr. Thackeray, he takes a peculiar pleasure in showing the contrariety between thought and speech, the heart within and the mask without, which we call a face. He is always showing that we are better than we seem, greater than we know, nearer to each other than, perhaps, we would wish. It is a fertile theme of immense interest, and through the three volumes the author has handled it with rare skill. . . .   [E. S. DALLAS]

The Athenaeum, 26 February 1859

'Adam Bede' is a novel of the highest class. Full of quiet power, without exaggeration and without any strain after effect, it produces a deep impression on the reader, which remains long after the book is closed. It is as though he had made acquaintance with real human beings: the story is not a story, but a true account of a place and people who have really lived; indeed, some of them may even be living yet, though they will be rather old, but that everything happened as here set down we have no doubt in the world. The duty of a critic in the present instance is almost superseded by the reader. 'Adam Bede' is a book to be accepted, not criticized. . . . It is very seldom we are called on to deal with a book in which there is so little to qualify our praise.

[GERALDINE JEWSBURY]

The Quarterly Review, October 1860

(A review of G.E.'s first three books)

. . . That all this [Hetty's journey] is represented with extraordinary force we need not say; and doubtless the partisans of 'George Eliot' would tell us that Scott could not have written the chapters in question. We do not think it necessary to discuss that point, but we are sure that in any case he *would* not have written them, because his healthy judgment would have rejected such matters as unfit for the novelist's art. . . .

The idea that fiction should contain something to soothe, to elevate or to purify seems to be extinct. In its stead there is a love for what would be better left in obscurity; for portraying the wildness of passion and the harrowing miseries of mental conflict; for dark pictures of sin and remorse and punishment; for the discussion of those questions which it is painful and revolting to think of. . . .   [REV. J. C. ROBERTSON]

Letter from E. Hall

(Transcribed in G.E.'s *Journal*, February 1859)

To the Author of 'Adam Bede.'

CHESTER ROAD, SUNDERLAND

DEAR SIR,—I got the other day a hasty read of your 'Scenes of Clerical Life,' and since that a glance at your 'Adam Bede,' and was delighted more than I can express; but being a poor man, and having enough to do to make 'ends meet,' I am unable to get a read of your inimitable books.

Forgive, dear sir, my boldness in asking you to give us a cheap edition. You would confer on us a great boon. I can get plenty of trash for a few pence, but I am sick of it. I felt so different when I shut your books, even though it was but a kind of 'hop, skip, and jump' read.

I feel so strongly in this matter, that I am determined to risk being thought rude and officious, and write to you.

Many of my working brethren feel as I do, and I express their wish as well as my own. Again asking your forgiveness for intruding myself upon you—I remain, with profoundest respect, yours, &c.,

E. Hall

The Westminster Review, October 1876

(This review of *Daniel Deronda* prefaced its unfavourable notice of the book with a leisurely survey of G.E.'s other novels, and selected Hetty Sorrel as one of her masterpieces)

... The figure of Hetty is like nothing that art had before developed out of nature, and yet it is profoundly true, with a reality in it which makes the heart ache. The very landscape, hitherto so broad and large and calm, changes and intensifies round this being, so tragical in her levity and shallowness. Never was the hapless simpleton, strange mixture of innocence and that self-love which is the root of ill, deserving of her fate, yet not deserving, in her lightness and reckless ignorance, of any such tremendous encounter with destiny and the powers of evil, so wonderfully set forth. In most cases, when a human soul, either in history or fiction, is brought face to face with the darker passions and calamities, it is of a nature lofty enough to cope with and combat them; but George Eliot was the first to thrill the spectator with the sight of a helpless, frivolous, childish creature, inadequate even to under-

stand, much less to contend with, those gigantic shadows, con-
fronted all at once by despair, crime, remorse, and destruction—
things with which her soft childlike foolishness and baby character
had nothing to do. The effect produced is much like that which
would be roused in us did we see a child set in motion, by some
heedless touch, a whole system of grim machinery, such as must
crush it into a thousand pieces, and before which we stand trembling
and appalled, not only by the horror itself, but by the shock of
those tremendous forces employed for such a result. The anguish
of pity in such a case is not mingled with any of those nobler
sentiments which make the heart swell when we watch a worthy
struggle, but is sharp and sore with our inability to assist, and with
yearning over the helpless victim. There is nothing finer in modern
literature than the power with which this contrast is kept up, and
the slightness and frivolity of poor Hetty's being, preserved consistent through all the tempest of woe that comes upon her. A
lesser artist would have made this trifling country girl develop
into a heroine in face of the terrible emergency; but genius knows
better; and the tragedy gains in depth and solemn force from the
helpless weakness of the central figure. We have seen a spotless
Desdemona, a lovely dream like Juliet perish with a less pang and
shiver of feeling than that with which we watch this poor, pretty,
self-regarding fool crouch helpless and dumb before the awful
fates. . . .

From *The Life of H.R.H. The Prince Consort*
(vol. IV), Theodore Martin, 1879

(Quoted in *Blackwood's Magazine*, May 1879)

. . . All novels of character had for him an irresistible charm; and
none, therefore, took a greater hold upon his imagination and
memory than the early masterpieces of George Eliot, with which he
became acquainted a few months after this time. He revelled in
her humour, and the sayings of Mrs Poyser especially were often
on his lips, and quoted with an aptness which brought out their
significance with added force. So highly did he think of *Adam
Bede* that he sent a copy of it to Baron Stockman soon after it
was published. 'It will amuse you,' he said in the letter sending it,
'by the fullness of variety of its studies of human character.'. . .

⁋ Praise of *Adam Bede* was almost universal, and it was also a great success commercially: 3,000 copies were sold in the first three months, and it went on selling steadily for years. During her lifetime, it was the most popular of George Eliot's novels, and the *Quarterly* reviewer of 1876 is not the only critic to use it as a stick to beat the later novels. Today this judgement is universally reversed: partly for the positive reason that we have learned to appreciate the later masterpieces so fully, and partly for the negative reason that we have lost our taste for the sort of book George Eliot was writing in *Adam Bede*. The kindliness, the high view of human nature, so praised by *The Times*, is eagerly scrutinised for sentimentality by the modern reader, and if he acquits it he will do so without enthusiasm. The book's undoubted faults— the patronising tone of its asides, the streak of melodrama towards the end—are those which the Victorians found easiest to forgive, and which offend us most readily. Its undoubted merits—the charm and realism of the rural setting, the nutty wisdom, the shrewd generosity—are those which the twentieth century has to teach itself to value. It is not surprising, then, that contemporaries received *Adam Bede* with such (to us) uncritical admiration.

The one part of the book which needs no apology to modern taste is the journey of Hetty: to Windsor in search of her lover, then home in despair. It is by far the finest thing in *Adam Bede*: compassionate but starkly honest, universalised and desperately moving. As if to confirm that the whirligig of taste brings in his revenges, we find this very part singled out for condemnation in the *Quarterly*. It is not often that changes of literary principle can be so clearly illustrated: this reviewer has seen what we see, has (one suspects) been moved by it as we are, but our praise is his condemnation. He was old-fashioned even in 1860; and only sixteen years later (though admittedly in the more up-to-date *Westminster Review*) we find another critic praising the same journey: praising it in rather dated rhetoric, but with criteria that are surely quite acceptable to us.

III · THE MILL ON THE FLOSS

❡ *The Mill on the Floss* was written during 1859 and the first months of 1860, and was published on 4 April 1860.

The Spectator, 7 April 1860

... The awakening of the girl's higher faculties under the influence of a mind of wider range and finer tone than her own is indicated, and the effect of the circumstances of her childhood and youth on her manners, speech, and actions, is shown so naturally, that one for a time quite forgets the artist and her art. Maggie is no exceptional girl in any way; far, far removed from the 'faultless monster' of the old romance, and still as far from the pale, clever, and sharp-spoken young woman whom *Jane Eyre* made fashionable for a time. A woman's natural impulses; all the wild fancies and self-torturing thoughts of a young girl vivid in imagination, but not strong in any mental exercise, and obliged to live a life at first very narrow, and then very mean—are described exactly as they might happen, as they do happen, in thousands of English homes. The novelty and interest lie in the fact that in very few works of fiction has the interior of the mind been so keenly analysed. We had such an analysis in *Jane Eyre*, powerful and distinct for evermore to all who read that great story; but Jane Eyre was no ordinary young woman; she was exceptional in circumstances, exceptional in her own nature. Maggie Tulliver is not exceptional; the wayward little child, 'naughty' to the last degree, quick in her 'ways,' is natural enough, and the growth of her characteristics bears all the impress of the facts around her. ...

There are parts of the story where the style gives a kind of consciousness of reality, as if you heard the words spoken by a voice shaken with the emotions so well described; there are passages of dialogue where the love between men and women is expressed more naturally and powerfully, we think, than in any novel we ever read. Rising fresh from the perusal, we may over-rate the power of these passages, and attribute to style or words what may be due to situations the interest of which is prepared by skilful construction; but we think there can be no mistaking the wondrous human passion that animates the scenes between the two lovers—bound to others in honour, yet clinging together with such appealing love. . . .

In this novel, therefore, we have reproduced the old grand element of interest which the Greek drama possessed, the effect of circumstances upon man; but you have, in addition, that analysis of the inner mind, of which *Hamlet* stands in literature the greatest example. In the case of Maggie, we have a career regarded both from the inside and from the outside; we feel the throbbing of her heart at each new sensation, and we see, as it were, from our own stand-point, the outward facts that awaken her to new life. On sweeps the river of life and of destiny; the flood resistless, the waters strong: men and homes, and old associations of outer life, are swept away for miles, or engulphed; all around drifts from its moorings; and, as spectators, we watch the roll of the resistless tide. On comes one young girl, alone upon a raft, hardly saved from the flood; she strives against the current, but is still swept along, and now we are made conscious of her thoughts and feelings. We see not alone the river of life, with its hard facts floated away, and its merciless waters, but we are conscious of every thought of the victim. We follow back to the heart the retreating blood that has left the cheek pale; we know every gleam of hope and pang of despair that runs through mind and soul, as the familiar landmarks are passed, and she is drifted down with the flood. We do not remember any novel where the interest so clearly centres round the one character, where every fact—the smallest—is read with deep attention, because it may affect her—as in real life the very name of a town or street, or even shop, remembered in connexion with some one person much beloved, has at once a new vivid life. Not that Maggie is made actually powerful in her influence on the other persons, but that everything she does, or anything done to her, is of interest, and thus the whole story takes a noble unity.

Sterne eulogized critics who were pleased 'they knew not why, and cared not wherefore.' In the present day, we are perhaps unhappily too critical to be satisfied with that simple and gracious reception of great works of art. We cannot help analysing the mechanism of this great story. It seems to us that the first idea was simply what we have indicated—the onward 'storm and stress' of the soul, the outward rush and plash of the river of life on which it is swept along. It is with great joy that we recognize the consummate art with which this idea is worked out. The smallest details worked in help to make the idea real. There is even in the material facts a half-hidden symbolism indicating the idea of the story. When Maggie tells Philip Wakem why she loves her brother, she thinks that it was holding his hand she first saw the rushing water of the floss. The quarrel about the water privileges affects her whole life. She is carried away by the flood out to sea with the man she loves and must not love, and where her physical danger and her moral peril are brought close together. Finally, the catastrophe comes as the river of life overwhelms her, and the symbolism is complete. The beauty of this under-current of symbolism is that it is unexpressed, but the mere material facts of the river playing such a great part in Maggie's life give one the feeling that she is swept along by a current of circumstances she can neither resist nor control.

We might dwell on minor beauties; but we have lingered too long over our task. Inferior to *Adam Bede* in the varied interest of three or four good characters, it is superior as a work of art; with a higher aim and that aim more artistically worked out.

The Saturday Review, 14 April 1860

. . . She is full of meditation on some of the most difficult problems of life. She occupies herself with the destinies, the possibilities, and the religious position of all the people of whom she cares to think. Especially she seems haunted with the thoughts of the amazing discrepancy between what she calls 'the emmet-life' of these British farmers, and the ideal of Christianity. She dwells on the pettiness, the narrowness, the paganism of their character. She even takes a pleasure in making the contrast as strong as she can. In her stern determination to paint what she conceives to be the truth, to soften nothing and not to exalt and elevate where she profoundly believes all to be poor and low, she shocks us with traits of character that are exceptional, however possible. In the *Mill on the Floss* an old miller is ruined, and the fault, as he thinks, lies at the door of a roguish lawyer. When he finds his ruin is accomplished, he solemnly takes the family Bible, and in the flyleaf records a curse against his enemy. Usually, however, the proceedings of the Dodsons and their set are much milder. It is the gossip, the stinginess, the total absence of all spirituality in the farmer circles that weigh upon George Eliot. She has set herself to imagine how such influences would tell upon an exception to the set, in a lively, imaginative, impulsive girl, the daughter of the Dodson married to the miller. The history of this girl is taken up when she is seven years old, and is continued until she has been for some time a young woman. She goes through great outward trials, in addition to the perpetual suffering inflicted on her by relations who entirely misunderstand her. She has a period in which fiction is everything to her, and she consoles herself for all that reality imposes on her by the delightful dreams of the imagination. When her suffering becomes too intense, she takes refuge in mystical religion. Later on, she seems to accept the doctrine inculcated by one of her lovers, that resignation cannot be the highest end of human life, as it is merely negative. She then passes into a stage where she is absorbed in the fierce moral conflicts awakened by a passion to which she thinks it wrong to yield. All this is entirely in the vein of Charlotte Bronté, and the *Mill on the Floss* shows that George Eliot has thought as keenly and profoundly as the authoress of *Jane Eyre* on the peculiar difficulties and sorrows encountered by a girl of quick feeling and high aspirations under adverse outward circumstances. But the objection which we feel to difficult moral problems being handled in fiction is certainly not removed by the writings of either of these gifted women. What does it all come to except that human life is inexplicable, and that women who feel this find the feeling painful? It is true that a girl like the heroine of the *Mill on the Floss* is not an improbable character. Many a girl in the obscurity of an uncongenial home has first taken to ascetic and mystical religion, and then had doubts forced on her whether such a religion could give her peace. But because they really occur, it does not follow that spiritual doubts and conflicts are a proper subject for a novelist. Fiction has, in such matters, the great defect that it encourages both the writer and the reader to treat the most solemn problems of human life as things that are to be started, discussed, and laid aside at pleasure. The conduct of the story always affords an opening to escape from the responsibility of definite thought. It does even more than afford an opening—it forces the mind to escape from reflection into the study of outward life. The subjects started are, therefore, always too large for the

manner in which they are handled. When women like George Eliot
and Currer Bell are writing, we are perhaps too interested in their
style, in the freshness of their thoughts, and in the story they are
telling, to care much for the abandonment of the moral difficulties
that have been raised. But no one who considers how much harm
the light, trifling, and inadequate discussion of great subjects does
in the present day, can have much pleasure in finding that a
novelist powerful enough to become the example and excuse of
lesser writers exhibits ascetic religion as a temporary phase in a
young woman's career. . . .

The Leader, 14 April 1860

The authoress's intention in the present production must not be
mistaken. She has concentrated all the powers of her mind upon
the realization of an undeniable theory, namely, that the rare gifts
of a lively fancy and fertile imagination are fatal to the possessor
unless accompanied by the strength of mind and moral culture
necessary to hold them in subjection. Poor Maggie, the heroine of
this story, is presented to us as an instance of the truth of this
proposition. Born of parents utterly incapable of comprehending
the complicated subtleties of a nature so alien to their own, she is
looked upon by all connected with her as an ill weed, destined to
bring misery upon herself and those concerned in her proceedings.
Her impulsive character leads her into eccentricities, for which no
allowance is made by her prejudiced family; in vain she strives to
do right; she is sure, by some unforeseen accident, or unhappy
bungling in her mode of accomplishing it, to bring about the very
opposite to what she intends; the consequence is, that her childhood is passed amid continual upbraidings, bickerings, and strife.
This is the more trying to our heroine, as the love and approbation
of others is one of the great needs of her peculiar disposition. She
yearns for affection with an eagerness of appetite that gains fresh
intensity, from the fact that few or no attempts are made to
appease it. She is left entirely to herself, to the formation of her
own regulating principles, and development of her own mental
faculties. Can it be wondered that, with such an imperfect education, Maggie should grow up a creature of wild and contradictory
impulses, possessing grand and sterling qualities of heart, firm in
her resolve to master her own weaker passions, but ever precipitat-
ing herself into evil by the errors of her judgment? . . .

The Atlas, 14 April 1860

... The notion of predestined calamity, though never brought prominently forward, is vaguely hinted at from the commencement and never lost sight of throughout the narrative. A unity and completeness of effect is thus attained, as rare as it is excellent. The story opens with a description of the water-mill on the borders of the river Floss, and the key note is at once struck, which first comes trembling on the ear, then increases in its ominous sound, till it shatters two lives in its reverberating shock. We are first introduced to the mill-owner through 'a great curtain of sound,' caused by the 'rush of the water and the booming of the mill:' it is the water which has a special attraction for Tom and Maggie; the law-suit consequent on a fancied infringement of Mr. Tulliver's share of water-power ends in his ruin; again, the water is the medium for the elopement of Maggie with her cousin's suitor: and it is the water, in its flooded rage, close to the old mill, which brings swift justice and everlasting rest to brother and sister. In all this, the hand of the artist is apparent. . . .

The Sun, 23 April 1860

... Great tact and discrimination are displayed in the selection of the class of persons who figure before us in this eventful drama. They are taken from the ranks of the workers of the world, and yet the superior ones. To evidence the strongest passions, the darkest hatreds, the most critical junctures, the most bitter failures, to make wealth so gained that the sting of poverty is doubly felt, and to render connections so numerous that their subsequent desertion seems the culminating point of insult, where could the novelist seek better or find more powerful illustrations than among the middle ranks of society. Poverty, that has so many ills, has some advantages, it makes one of no consequence, and the lonely cot, and humble room, are, for the most part, unmolested by claimants or plotters. In higher walks of life, in pecuniary difficulties, or in disputes about succession to titles or holders of estates there would not enter all the thousand rancours and heart-burnings that envenom and empoison the dusty ways and crooked turnings of the busy tribes who are the medium in the scale of social gradations. . . .

opposite

The Guardian, 25 April 1860

The impressions of a reader of this book will probably vary in the progress of his reading. At first, the feeling will possibly be one of disappointment. With a full recognition of the keen observation and consummate exhibition of character, displayed in bringing out in living distinctness a set of well-to-do persons of the retired tradesman or higher farmer class, and their peculiar ideas about the duties and claims of relationship, there comes also the doubt whether all this was worth the painting, especially as they are all of them more or less disagreeable—persons whom we only like to read about, if we have the accompanying consciousness that we have nothing to do with any like them. But as the chapters go on, we begin to see that there is something more in view than a mere introduction to the domestic life, contrasts, and bickerings at Dorlcote Mill and Garum Firs. Greater interests—misfortune, disappointment, the sickness that lays low the ruined strong man, mingle with the details, still most completely and powerfully painted, of every-day life, shed their awful lights on what is weak and commonplace, give a touching interest to the distresses of trivial minds unable to rise to the height of their sorrow, and bring out in various new aspects the people whom we have only known in frugal and monotonous prosperity. We begin to feel the vigour of the narrator: we begin to feel that we have not been tempted, by the fame of *Adam Bede*, to what is but a mere curious and genial study of the still life, which goes on in the comfortable homes of the substantial population of the provinces. If we are a little disappointed that we have met with no one to delight in like Mrs. Poyser, we cannot help being sensible of a great variety of persons, quite new, and yet very familiar to us, with the most distinct marks of individuality in everything they say and do, whose action on one another's happiness and characters is followed out into all its complications, and all its results, touching and sad, as well as grotesquely comic. The story gains upon us in interest, not so much with reference as to what it is to end in, but because of the interweaving of the tragic elements, of human vicissitudes, and human ways of behaving under them, with what so undeniably belongs to the most homespun and unimaginative forms of English life. But we read on, and a remarkable change meets us. We have entered on entirely different scenery. We have left behind us the quiet country stream in its summer softness, or dull wintry chilliness, with its dipping willows and rumbling mill-wheel, and the modest and tidy and rather lifeless square houses beside it: and we are in a wide open estuary, with a wild sea rising and a lowering sky, broken by passing gleams and bursts of glorious sunset light, but with night coming on, and the dim and mysterious horizon of tossing water before us, and lines of white breakers not far off. We pass from the petty collisions and narrow thoughts of most ordinary farmers and tradesmen, delicately described, with an intense zest and humour in the process, to scenes where our interest is concentrated on struggles and conflicts of passion, faith and right, analysed with a glance which nothing escapes, and described with unsurpassed and terrible power. We pass from what amuses us with the oddities of life, and delights us still more by the skill which reproduces them so faithfully, to what awes us with a glimpse into the deepest questions, and the most tremendous realities of life, questions and realities about our temptations, our sins, and our destiny. With whatever reserves we may have to make, both as to the conduct and the substance of the story, our impulse at this concluding stage of it is to say that it is one of the grandest and most subduing, as it is one of the boldest pictures ever attempted, of the way in which the soul makes trials for itself, and of the unexplored depths of weakness and of strength, which temptation, as it becomes more intense and decisive, brings to light. . . .

Two faults strike us at once in this remarkable work. One is of structure. Nobody who reads it can, we should think, avoid the feeling that in the last volume he passes into a new book. There is a clear dislocation in the story, between Maggie's girlhood and Maggie's great temptation. It is perfectly true that it may be the same in real life. There was very likely a tranquil childhood previous to deeds or sufferings which have made the world ring. The commonplace trivialities and unmeaning events of life go on in their most unexciting course to the very eve and verge of the frightful catastrophe—the sudden death, the downfall of prosperity, the hopeless wreck of character and hope. But the actual course of human things is not necessarily the pattern for a work of art. A poem or a novel calls forth a certain group of feelings which seem to become its appropriate atmosphere; we read *Winter's Tale*, or the *Tempest*, in a different attitude of mind, with different associations of ideas, with different expectations as to the strings which are to be touched within us, from those with which we read *Hamlet* or *Othello*. We do not expect, and it is hardly pleasant, to be called in the same work from one set of thoughts, and, still more, one set of feelings, to another; to have them suddenly strained and screwed up; so that we hardly realise the scenes we were among a few chapters back. Nor is this incongruity avoided by the early interspersing of auguries and warnings of coming fate, which a second reading discovers, but which, if they were not passed unheeded, were certainly ineffectual in preparing us for what was to come, and for harmonising the two portions of the story.

Our other objection is a different one. Passion is one of the legitimate materials of the novelist. But he incurs deep responsibility by the way in which he treats it. And we cannot think that he does good service by bringing into clear and powerful light its perverted and unwholesome growths; by making seem probable a development of it which, on the data given us, is an improbable one. It goes against our sense of likelihood that Maggie, being what she is represented, could have been so fascinated by Stephen; certainly nothing is shown us in Stephen, except his own admiration for her, to account for it; and again, we must say that it is most improbable that if Maggie had strength to break her chain at the last and most difficult moment, she should not have had strength to break it before. Moral improbabilities are not atoned for by the power which softens them down and disguises them. But, however this be, the picture of passion gradually stealing like a frightful and incurable poison over not merely principle and self-respect, but even over that faith and honour to the unsuspecting and confiding which the very opinion of the world helps us to hold sacred—of the 'limed soul which, struggling to be free, is more engaged,' is one which had better never have been set before us with so much plainness. We will say at once that the writer never for an instant loses sight of the sin and the shame which she is describing. There may be a passage here and there which show how dangerous the subject is to meddle with. But there is nothing but warning in the result; the loss and the brave penitence, the incurable wound and the generous and humble acceptance of necessary chastisement, are more moving than many sermons. But fully allowing all this, we still hold that there are temptations which it is of itself a temptation to scrutinise too closely; conflicts in the conscience, which it only hardens us to contemplate, much more to do so in our idle hours—wrong doing and wrong feeling, which we are safer and happier in knowing only at a distance—

3

Non raggioniam di lor, ma guarda e passa.

And in this story, the boldness and power with which ultimate victory and recovery are held up before us are, practically, not a compensation for the equal power and boldness with which, secure of the final triumph of good, the writer has displayed in all its strength the force of evil, changing itself into ever new shapes, penetrating into the most unexpected recesses of the heart, starting up afresh after it seemed conquered, and sweeping two helpless souls before it, like an irresistible fate, up to the last and most improbable moment of rescue.

The Times, 19 May 1860

'George Eliot' is as great as ever. She has produced a second novel, equal to her first in power, although not in interest. As far as interest is concerned, indeed, it would have been exceedingly difficult to repeat the triumph of *Adam Bede*, in which the author contrived to paint the lily and to gild refined gold by adding the charm of a delightful philosophy to the pleasure of a good story. The reader will at once remember that he could not help liking all the characters in that history. The general influence of the book was to reconcile us to human nature, to make us think better of our fellow men, to make us feel that in the weakest there is something to be admired, in the worst something to be loved, to draw us nearer to each other by showing how completely we are one, and so to give us not only the temporary delight of listening to a pleasant tale, but also the permanent good of an increased sympathy with our kind. It was comparatively easy to excite our interest in the doings of persons towards whom we were led to entertain such friendly feelings. We treasured all their sayings, we watched eagerly all their movements, we were curious as to all their thoughts. The author, apparently afraid of repeating herself, and determined to avoid the imputation of representing the world as too good and sugary, now introduces us to a very different set of personages. A majority of the characters brought together in these three volumes are unpleasant companions—prosaic, selfish, nasty. We are launched into a world of pride, vain-glory, and hypocrisy, envy, hatred and malice, and all uncharitableness. Everybody is quarrelling with everybody in a small mean way; and we have the petty gossip and malignant slander of village worthies painted to the life. These are not promising materials, but the authoress has impressed her genius on them, and, relying on her marvellous powers of delineation, has felt that by the mere force of truth she could command our attention and compel applause. We doubt, indeed, whether Miss Lydia Languish will care much for this novel, and we are almost afraid to dwell on the nature of the theme which 'George Eliot' has chosen, lest the timid reader should be repulsed, and we should suggest an allusion to the supposed impossibility of making a silk purse out of a sow's ear. As to the fact that here we have the silk purse there can be no mistake, but it would require the genius of 'George Eliot' to describe by what magic it is produced out of materials that appear to be singularly barren of silk. . . .

The Dodson family are stingy, selfish wretches, who give no sympathy and require none, who would let a neighbour starve, and let a brother be bankrupt when a very little assistance would save him from the disgrace; but they would not touch a penny that is not theirs, there is no legal obligation which they would not discharge, they would scorn the approach of a lie. They would be truthful and honest, not as a social duty, but as a personal pride— because nobody should have it in his or her power to say that they were weak enough to neglect a manifest obligation. From the same source of self-satisfied strength comes pugnacity in all its forms of rivalry and contradiction, jealousies and criticisms, lawsuits, and slanders, and blows. Everybody in this tale is repelling everybody, and life is in the strictest sense a battle. Even the good angel of the story, that little Maggie, who is full of affection, and whose affection is continually leading her into blunders and misfortunes, is first of all introduced to us while she is indulging an unnatural ferocity towards her doll, whose head she is punching—driving a nail into it as Jael drove one into the temples of Sisera. Her brother Tom, who is the next important personage in the little community, is chiefly remarkable for self-assertion and hard-headed resistance of fate—his strong wrestling with adversity, and his anxiety to punish the slightest offence. Her father, Mr. Tulliver, is the incarnation of pugnacity. Her uncles and aunts are nothing if not critical, and after bickering among themselves for days together, and crowing over each other in the pride of imaginary conquest, look out upon their little parish with somewhat of the dissatisfaction which made the most renowned of victors lament that there were no more worlds to conquer. . . .

This life of proud self-assertion that on the bad side presents itself in an incessant bickering, and on the best side appears as a devotion to justice and truth for selfish ends, may become interesting by being made heroic. The Brontes—both Charlotte and Emily were fond of depicting this character, and by the account of Mrs. Gaskell, and by that of 'George Eliot,' it is a character that abounds in the northern counties. But when Charlotte or Emily Bronte dealt with such a nature, they ennobled or, at least, magnified it. In their pages we looked on men essentially selfish and unsociable—men encased in armour of proof against all encroachment—men who wronged nobody, and who vowed that nobody should wrong them. But the selfish isolation of such characters was lit up with passion, was justified or expiated by long suffering from some overwhelming wrong, was idealized by being joined to the possession of great intellectual powers. 'George Eliot' has attempted a more difficult task. She takes these characters as we find them in real life—in all their intrinsic littleness. She paints them as she finds them—snapping at each other over the tea-table; eyeing each other enviously at church; privately plotting how to astonish each other by some extraordinary display; putting the worst construction on every word and act; officiously proffering advice and predicting calamity; living with perfect content their sordid life of vulgar respectability. The first half of the novel is devoted to the exhibition of this degraded species of existence, which is dissected with a masterly hand. Although it is the least exciting part of the work, it is the part of which the reader will carry away the most vivid recollection. The Dodson family will live for ever, and they inspire the work. With a self-denial which we cannot but admire, the author has resolutely set herself the task of delineating, without exaggeration, without extenuation, with minute accuracy, the sort of life which thousands upon thousands of our countrymen lead—a life that outwardly is most respectable, but inherently is most degraded—so degraded, indeed, that the very virtues which adorn it are scarcely to be distinguished from vices. . . .   [E. S. DALLAS]

The National Review, July 1860

. . . It is when we come to the third volume, which is intended to portray the effect on Maggie of an irresistible and yet unhappy and unworthy passion, her conflict with it, the moral problems to which it leads, and her ultimate victory over it,—that we seem

to lose sight at once of the artistic power of the author, and of
the delicate moral discrimination which is so conspicuous in
Adam Bede.

And let us say at once that we do not believe that this tale adopts
or embodies any questionable moral principle. The charge which
we bring against it is not that of asserting false principles, or failing
to assert true ones. The painful impression produced is due entirely
to the interpolation into the picture of a noble though not faultless
character,—of an episode so inconsistent with its general tenor, as
to force on us the conviction that the author does not believe any
amount of native fidelity and delicacy of character powerful enough
to protect her heroine against the overmastering fascination of what
she calls the 'law of attraction.' She evidently estimates all the
natural safeguards which position, duty, and feeling in a refined
and delicate nature can impose as utterly inadequate to defend
her against the approaches of physical passion. She enthrones
physiological law so far above both affections and conscience in
point of *strength*, that she represents Maggie as drifting helplessly
into a vortex of passion, and rescued at last only by the last
spasmodic effort of a nearly overpowered will.

Maggie is staying with her cousin Lucy, to whom she is tenderly
attached. Her cousin is known to be all but engaged to Mr. Stephen
Guest, while she herself is pledged at heart to Philip Wakem. But
the *idea*, if it can be so called, of this unpleasant part of the book is,
that a powerful physique, and the self-possessed nature which
rarely goes with a diseased or delicate physique, is an essential to
command the full passion of Maggie's heart, which Mr. Stephen
Guest strives for and obtains. The man is a pinchbeck hero,—not
of sterling metal at all; indeed, the sketch of him is poor, and
does not even realise him strongly to our minds. But the grave
fault of the episode is the assumption that the ingrained affectionateness and fidelity of Maggie's nature should be no protection
against the approaches of her quite *unmotived* passion for Lucy's
lover. It must be remembered that, whatever were the defects of
the social influences under which she is represented as having been
educated, an intense regard for the claims of kindred and the
claims of justice are depicted as deeply rooted in all her relations.
This feeling is painted as reproduced in full force both in brother
and sister; and yet it never even occurs to the author that these
deeply implanted principles would have exercised so powerful a
latent effect as to counteract effectually any 'elective affinities'

between her and Mr. Guest. The whole of this portion of the book is a kind of enthusiastic homage to physiological law, and seems to us as untrue to nature as it is unpleasant and indelicate. The light of a character in itself transparently beautiful is here almost extinguished in very unfragrant fumes of physiological smoke. . . .

Macmillan's Magazine, April 1861

. . . So far as exquisite literary skill, informed and vivified by the highest order of imaginative power, can go, this story is perfect. But take it from another point of view. Ask, what good will it do? —whether it will lighten any burdened heart, help any perplexed spirit, comfort the sorrowful, succour the tempted, or bring back the erring into the way of peace; and what is the answer? Silence.

Let us reconsider the story, not artistically, but morally.

Here is a human being, placed during her whole brief life—her hapless nineteen years—under circumstances the hardest and most fatal that could befall one of her temperament. She has all the involuntary egotism and selfishness of a nature that, while eagerly craving for love, loves ardently and imaginatively rather than devotedly; and the only love that might have at once humbled and raised her, by showing her how far nobler it was than her own —Philip's—is taken from her in early girlhood. Her instincts of right, true as they are, have never risen into principles; her temptations to vanity, and many other faults, are wild and fierce; yet no human help ever comes near her to strengthen the one or subdue the other. This *may* be true to nature, and yet we think it is not. Few of us, calmly reviewing our past, can feel that we have ever been left so long and so utterly without either outward aid, or the inner voice—never silent in a heart like poor *Maggie's*. It is, in any case, a perilous doctrine to preach—the doctrine of over-powering circumstances.

Again, notwithstanding the author's evident yearning over *Maggie*, and disdain for *Tom*, we cannot but feel that if people are to be judged by the only fair human judgment, of how far they act up to what they believe in, *Tom*, so far as his light goes, is a finer character than his sister. He alone has the self-denial to do what he does not like, for the sake of doing right; he alone has the self-command to smother his hopeless love, and live on, a brave, hard-working life; he, except in his injustice to poor *Maggie*, has at least the merit of having made no one else miserable. Perfectly true is what he says, though he says it in a Pharisaical way, 'Yes, *I* have had feelings to struggle with, but I conquered them. I have had a harder life than you have had, but I have found *my* comfort in doing my duty.' Nay, though perhaps scarcely intended, Bob Jakin's picture of the solitary lad, 'as close as an iron biler,' who 'sits by himself so glumpish, a-knittin' his brow, an' a-lookin' at the fire of a night,' is in its way as pathetic as *Maggie's* helpless cry to Dr. Kenn, at the bazaar, 'O, I must go.'

In the whole history of this fascinating *Maggie* there is a picturesque piteousness which somehow confuses one's sense of right and wrong. Yet what—we cannot help asking—what is to become of the hundreds of clever girls, born of uncongenial parents, hemmed in with unsympathising kindred of the Dodson sort, blest with no lover on whom to bestow their strong affections, no friend to whom to cling for guidance and support? They must fight their way, heaven help them! alone and unaided, through cloud and darkness, to the light. And, thank heaven, hundreds of them do, and live to hold out a helping hand afterwards to thousands more. 'The middle-aged' (says 'George Eliot,' in this very book), 'who have lived through their strongest emotions, but are yet in the time when memory is still half-passionate and not merely contemplative, should surely be a sort of natural priesthood, whom life has disciplined and consecrated to be the refuge and rescue of early stumblers and victims of self-despair.'

Will it help these—such a picture as *Maggie*, who, with all her high aspirations and generous qualities, is, throughout her poor young life, a stay and comfort to no human being, but, on the contrary, a source of grief and injury to every one connected with her? If we are to judge character by results—not by grand imperfect essays, but by humbler fulfilments—of how much more use in the world were even fond, shallow *Lucy*, and narrow-minded *Tom*, than this poor *Maggie*, who seems only just to have caught hold of the true meaning and beauty of existence in that last pathetic prayer, 'If my life is to be long, let me live to bless and comfort,' when she is swept away out of our sight and love for ever.

True this is, as we have said, a magnificent ending for the book; but is it for the life—the one human life which this author has created so vividly and powerfully, that we argue concerning it as if we had actually known it? Will it influence for good any other real lives—this passionately written presentment of temptation never conquered, or just so far that we see its worst struggle as but beginning; of sorrows which teach nothing, or teach only bitterness; of love in its most delicious, most deadly phase; love blind, selfish, paramount, seeing no future but possession, and, that hope gone, no alternative but death—death, welcomed as the solution of all difficulties, the escape from all pain?

Is this right? Is it a creed worthy of an author who has preeminently what all novelists should have, 'the brain of a man and the heart of a woman,' united with what we may call a sexless intelligence, clear and calm, able to observe, and reason, and guide mortal passions, as those may, who have come out of the turmoil of the flesh into the region of ministering spirits, 'αγγελοι,' messengers between God and man? What if the messenger testify falsely? What if the celestial trumpet give forth an uncertain sound?

Yet let us be just. There are those who argue that this—perhaps the finest ending, artistically, of any modern novel, is equally fine in a moral sense: that the death of *Maggie* and *Tom* is a glorious Euthanasia, showing that when even at the eleventh hour, temptation is conquered, error atoned, and love reconciled, the life is complete: its lesson has been learnt, its work done; there is nothing more needed but the *vade in pacem* to an immediate heaven. This, if the author so meant it, was an idea grand, noble, Christian: as Christian (be it said with reverence) as the doctrine preached by the Divine Pardoner of all sinners to the sinner beside whom He died—'To-day shalt thou be with me in paradise.' But the conception ought to have been worked out so plainly that no reader could mistake it. We should not have been left to feel, as we do feel, undecided whether this death was a translation or an escape: whether if they had not died, *Maggie* would not have been again the same *Maggie*, always sinning and always repenting; and *Tom* the same *Tom*, hard and narrow-minded, though the least ray of love and happiness cast over his gloomy life, might have softened and made a thoroughly good man of him. The author ought to have satisfied us entirely as to the radical change in both; else we fall back upon the same dreary creed of overpowering circumstances: of human beings struggling for ever in a great quagmire of unconquerable temptations, inevitable and hopeless woe. A creed more fatal to every noble effort, and brave self-restraint—above all to that humble faith in the superior Will which alone should govern ours—can hardly be conceived. It is true that there occur sometimes in life positions so complex and overwhelming, that plain right and wrong become confused; until the most righteous and religious man is hardly able to judge clearly or act fairly. But to meet such positions is one thing, to *invent* them is another. It becomes a serious question whether any author—who, great as his genius may be, sees no farther than mortal intelligence can—is justified in leading his readers into a labyrinth, the way out of which he does not, first, see clearly himself, and next, is able to make clear to them, so as to leave them mentally and morally at rest, free from all perplexity and uncertainty. . . .

It is *not* right to paint *Maggie* only as she is in her strong, unsatisfied, erring youth—and leave her there, her doubts unresolved, her passions unregulated, her faults unatoned and unforgiven: to cut her off ignobly and accidentally, leaving two acts, one her recoil of conscience with regard to *Stephen*, and the other her instinctive self-devotion in going to rescue *Tom*, as the sole noble landmarks of a life that had in it every capability for good with which a woman could be blessed. It is *not* right to carry us on through these three marvellous volumes, and leave us at the last standing by the grave of the brother and sister, ready to lift up an accusatory cry, less to a beneficent Deity than to the humanly-invented Arimanes of the universe.—'Why should such things be? Why hast Thou made us thus?'

But it may be urged, that fiction has its counterpart, and worse, in daily truth. How many perplexing histories do we not know of young lives blighted, apparently by no fault of their own; of blameless lives dragged into irresistible temptations; of high natures so meshed in by circumstances that they, as well as we, judging them from without, can hardly distinguish right from wrong, guilt from innocence; of living and loveable beings so broken down by unmerited afflictions, that when at last they come to an end, we look on the poor dead face with a sense of thankfulness that there at least,

> 'There is no other thing expressed
> But long disquiet merged in rest.'

All this is most true, *so far as we see*. But we never can see, not even the wisest and greatest of us, anything like *the whole* of even the meanest and briefest human life. We never can know through what fiery trial of temptation, nay, even sin,—for sin itself appears sometimes in the wonderful alchemy of the universe to be used as an agent for good,—a strong soul is being educated into a saintly minister to millions of weaker souls: coming to them with the authority of one whom suffering has taught how to heal suffering; nay, whom the very fact of having sinned once, has made more deeply to pity, so as more easily to rescue sinners. And, lastly, we never can comprehend, unless by experience, that exceeding peace —the 'peace which passeth all understanding,' which is oftentimes seen in those most heavily and hopelessly afflicted: those who have lost all, and gained their own souls: whereof they possess themselves in patience: waiting until the 'supreme moment' of which our author speaks, but which is to them not an escape from the miseries of this world, but a joyful entrance into the world everlasting.

Ay, thank heaven, though the highest human intellect may fail to hear it, there are millions of human hearts yet living and throbbing, or mouldering quietly into dust, who have felt, all through the turmoil or silence of existence, though lasting for threescore years and ten, a continual still small voice, following them to the end: 'Fear not: for I am thy GOD.'

Would that in some future book, as powerful as '*The Mill on the Floss*,' the author might become a true '*Ἀγγελος*,' and teach us this!

The Atlantic Monthly, October 1866

'The Novels of George Eliot'

... Of the four English studies, *The Mill on the Floss* seems to me to have most dramatic continuity, in distinction from that descriptive, discursive method of narration which I have attempted to indicate. After Hetty Sorrel, I think Maggie Tulliver the most successful of the author's young women, and after Tito Melema, Tom Tulliver the best of her young men. English novels abound in pictures of childhood; but I know of none more truthful and touching than the early pages of this work. Poor erratic Maggie is worth a hundred of her positive brother, and yet on the very threshold of life she is compelled to accept him as her master. He falls naturally into the man's privilege of always being in the right. The following scene is more than a reminiscence; it is a real retrospect. Tom and Maggie are sitting upon the bough of an elder-tree, eating jam-puffs. At last only one remains, and Tom undertakes to divide it.

'The knife descended on the puff, and it was in two; but the result was not satisfactory to Tom, for he still eyed the halves doubtfully. At last he said, "Shut your eyes, Maggie."

'"What for?"

'"You never mind what for,—shut 'em when I tell you."

'Maggie obeyed.

'"Now, which'll you have, Maggie, right hand or left?"

'"I'll have that one with the jam run out," said Maggie, keeping her eyes shut to please Tom.

'"Why, you don't like that, you silly. You may have it if it comes to you fair, but I sha'n't give it to you without. Right or left, —you choose now. Ha-a-a!" said Tom, in a tone of exasperation, as Maggie peeped. "You keep your eyes shut now, else you sha'n't have any."

'Maggie's power of sacrifice did not extend so far; indeed, I fear she cared less that Tom should enjoy the utmost possible amount of puff, than that he should be pleased with her for giving him the best bit. So she shut her eyes quite close until Tom told her to "say which," and then she said, "Left hand."

'"You've got it," said Tom, in rather a bitter tone.

'"What! the bit with the jam run out?"

'"No; here, take it," said Tom, firmly, handing decidedly the best piece to Maggie.

'"O, please, Tom, have it; I don't mind,—I like the other; please take this."

'"No, I shan't," said Tom, almost crossly, beginning on his own inferior piece.

'Maggie, thinking it was of no use to contend further, began too, and ate up her half puff with considerable relish as well as rapidity. But Tom had finished first, and had to look on while Maggie ate her last morsel or two, feeling in himself a capacity for more. *Maggie didn't know Tom was looking at her: she was see-sawing on the elder-bough, lost to everything but a vague sense of jam and idleness.*

'"O, you greedy thing!" said Tom, when she had swallowed the last morsel.'

The portions of the story which bear upon the Dodson family are in their way not unworthy of Balzac; only that, while our author has treated its peculiarities humourously, Balzac would have treated them seriously, almost solemnly. We are reminded of him by the attempt to classify the Dodsons socially in a scientific manner, and to accumulate small examples of their idiosyncrasies. I do not mean to say that the resemblance is very deep.

The chief defect—indeed, the only serious one—in *The Mill on the Floss* is its conclusion. Such a conclusion is in itself assuredly not illegitimate, and there is nothing in the fact of the flood, to my knowledge, essentially unnatural: what I object to is its relation to the preceding part of the story. The story is told as if it were destined to have, if not a strictly happy termination, at least one within ordinary probabilities. As it stands, the *dénouement* shocks the reader most painfully. Nothing has prepared him for it; the story does not move towards it; it casts no shadow before it. Did such a *dénouement* lie within the author's intentions from the first, or was it a tardy expedient for the solution of Maggie's difficulties? This question the reader asks himself, but of course he asks it in vain.

For my part, although, as long as humanity is subject to floods and earthquakes, I have no objection to see them made use of in novels, I would in this particular case have infinitely preferred that Maggie should have been left to her own devices. I understand the author's scruples, and to a certain degree I respect them. A lonely spinsterhood seemed but a dismal consummation of her generous life; and yet, as the author conceives, it was unlikely that she would return to Stephen Guest. I respect Maggie profoundly; but nevertheless I ask, Was this after all so unlikely? I will not try to answer the question. I have shown enough courage in asking it. But one thing is certain: a *dénouement* by which Maggie should have called Stephen back would have been extremely interesting, and would have had far more in its favour than can be put to confusion by a mere exclamation of horror. . . .   HENRY JAMES

❡ 'The first great fault in The Mill on the Floss,' declared the critic of *The Atlas*, 'is want of interest in the story or in any of the principal characters represented.' There would not seem to be much left to praise after that, but, having found fault for the first half of his review, he then went on to show the book's merits. Our extract (a proto-New Critical discussion of thematic imagery) is from this second half.

Most of the reviewers liked the book, and many had some fault to find (though not often as severely as *The Atlas*). The critic of *The Saturday Review*, though he believed the novel showed no falling-off of power, predicted that it would not be as popular as *Adam Bede*. He was right on both counts.

The Mill on the Floss stands out among George Eliot's novels as the one with which she was most closely involved emotionally. It is not an autobiographical novel in its events: Maggie's story is nothing like Marian Evans's. But in a more important sense it is deeply autobiographical: Maggie's struggles *are* her author's, transposed into fiction. Marian too had a brother whom she loved intensely as a child, who grew up conventional and self-righteous, and whom she quarrelled and broke with. She too went through a phase of violent asceticism and was constantly tempted by self-denial. She had the same passionate nature, the same need to be loved, the same instability, the same sublimated egoism, the same devoted loyalty.

Such identification with the heroine can be a source of strength or weakness to a novel. Strength because it breathes life into it, raises the emotional level and invites *our* identification: such novels are seldom dull or academic. Weakness because it unsteadies the judgement, and leads to an uncritical acceptance of the heroine's view of herself. Modern critics of *The Mill on the Floss* have thus tended to divide according to whether they approved or disapproved of the consequences of this identification; praising it for the vivid understanding of childhood and the sympathy for Maggie that burns through it, or criticising it for ending with (the words are F. R. Leavis's) 'the dreamed-of perfect accident that gives us the opportunity for the dreamed-of heroic act.' We can hardly expect such terminology in the Victorian critics, but they do divide in a very similar way. *The Spectator* finds the identification with Maggie an advantage: '... we feel the throbbing of her heart at each new sensation.' *The Saturday Review* regrets it (of course in more openly moral terms than a modern critic would allow himself), and fastens—like Leavis—on the ending: 'we are left undecided whether this death was a translation or an escape.' Perhaps 'translation' means much the same as Leavis's 'finality of great art', 'escape' much the same as his 'daydream indulgence'. And against both critics we can defend George Eliot by saying that her concern was to express powerfully and truthfully the ending she had chosen, not to choose another, morally preferable ending.

Yet all this gives us only one side of *The Mill on the Floss*. As well as a book of deep personal involvement, it is also one of

Objectivity

superb objectivity. George Eliot is one of the greatest of English social historians, and her description and analysis of the society of St Oggs shows a breadth of understanding beyond the range of most novelists. The most explicitly social comment among the reviews is that of the socialist periodical *The Sun*, which describes her subject-matter in more or less Marxist terms—terms not, perhaps, so alien to George Eliot's own thinking as we usually imagine.

The social analyst is almost inevitably a realist, in aim and method; and no term is commoner, in the reviews of George Eliot, than 'realism'—it is used both by those who praise and by those who blame. The complaint of *The Times*—that her subject-matter is unattractive—was to become more and more frequent; and perhaps no complaint can make us feel so strongly how far the mid-twentieth century is from the mid-nineteenth. After all that literature has dealt with in the last hundred years, denunciations of the Dodsons for their 'pride, vain-glory, and hypocrisy, envy, hatred and malice, and all uncharitableness' must make us sigh, in amused nostalgia, for a literature where *that* was the worst that had been shown of human nature.

Physical relations improper

In *The National Review* we find George Eliot castigated for being 'improper' in another and more familiar sense. Both *The Guardian* and *The Saturday Review* had already complained that physical passion was not a suitable subject for fiction. 'There are temptations,' wrote the *Guardian* critic, 'that it is of itself a temptation to scrutinise too closely'; and *The Saturday Review* included what was to become a common comparison with George Sand. No modern reader finds the treatment of sex in George Eliot outspoken, and our first impulse is, perhaps, to wish that it were. But reticence need not be a flaw in a novel: evasiveness is the flaw, and George Eliot is never evasive. Indeed, as *The National Review* reminds us, she was, by the standards of 1860, not even reticent.

There are few comments by George Eliot herself on her reviews, because she seldom read them. Her sensitive nature was easily discouraged, and she gratefully allowed her husband to act as a buffer—reading the notices, sometimes telling her about them, but not showing them to her. This system had not been completely adopted by the time of *The Mill on the Floss*, and so we have her reaction to two of these reviews. First, to *The Times*:

... The 'Times' article arrived on Sunday. It is written in a generous spirit, and with so high a degree of intelligence, that I am rather alarmed lest the misapprehensions it exhibits should be due to my defective presentation, rather than to any failure on the part of the critic. I have certainly fulfilled my intention very badly if I have made the Dodson honesty appear 'mean and uninteresting,' or made the payment of one's debts appear a contemptible virtue in comparison with any sort of 'Bohemian' qualities. So far as my own feeling and intention are concerned, no one class of persons or form of character is held up to reprobation or to exclusive admiration. Tom is painted with as much love and pity as Maggie; and I am so far from hating the Dodsons myself, that I am rather aghast to find them ticketed with such very ugly adjectives. . . .

[Letter to WILLIAM BLACKWOOD, 27 May 1860.]

❡ Her reaction to the *Macmillan's* article is more interesting. Being a thoroughly committed artist, she is sympathetic to the critic's moral approach, and her quarrel is rather with his views than his method. Her 'defence' of Tom raises a point of critical theory. With respect to this book, she is surely right: there is no failure of objectivity in her treatment of Tom. Yet is she not implicitly denying that we can ever accuse a novelist of failing to do justice to one of his own characters? Cases of unjust disdain are rare in G.E.; cases of damaging partiality (Felix Holt, Mordecai) are commoner:

... There is an article on 'The Mill' in 'Macmillan's Magazine' which is worth reading. I cannot, of course, agree with the writer in all his regrets: if I could have done so, I should not have written the book I did write, but quite another. Still it is a comfort to me to read any criticism which recognises the high responsibilities of literature that undertakes to represent life. The ordinary tone about art is that the artist may do what he will, provided he pleases the public. . . .

[Letter to JOHN BLACKWOOD, 30 March 1861.]

... And letters drop in from time to time giving me words of strong encouragement—especially about 'The Mill'; so that I have reason to be cheerful, and to believe that where one has a large public, one's words must hit their mark. If it were not for that, special cases of misinterpretation might paralyse me. For example, pray notice how one critic attributes to me a disdain for Tom; as if it were not *my* respect for Tom which infused itself into my reader,—as if he could have respected Tom if I had not painted him with respect; the exhibition of the right on both sides being the very soul of my intention in the story. However, I ought to be satisfied if I have roused the feeling that does justice to both sides.... [Letter to JOHN BLACKWOOD 4 April 1861.]

IV · SILAS MARNER

❦ *Silas Marner* was written between November 1860 and the
following March, and published 2 April 1861.

The Saturday Review, 13 April 1861

The highest tribute that can be paid to this book may be paid it
very readily. It is as good as *Adam Bede*, except that it is shorter.
And that an author should be able to produce a series of works so
good in so very peculiar a style, is as remarkable as anything that
has occurred in the history of English literature in this century.
The plot of *Silas Marner* is good, and the delineation of character
is excellent. But other writers who have the power of story-telling
compose plots as interesting, and perhaps sketch characters as well.
It is in the portraiture of the poor, and of what it is now fashionable to call 'the lower middle class,' that this writer is without a
rival, and no phase of life could be harder to draw. A person with
observation and humour might give a sketch of one or two sets of
poor people, and of village farmers and carpenters, but the sketches
he could give would be limited by his personal observation. George
Eliot alone moves among this unknown, and to most people
unknowable, section of society as if quite at home there, and can
let imagination run loose and disport itself in a field that, we think,
has been only very partially opened even to the best writers. Sir
Walter Scott drew a few pictures of humble Scotch life, and none
of his creations won him more deserved reputation than the
characters of Andrew Fairservice and Caleb Balderstone, and the
scenes among the poor fishing population in the *Antiquary*. But,
good as these sketches were, they were very limited. We soon got
to an end of them; but in *Silas Marner*, the whole book, or nearly
the whole book, is made up of such scenes. The writer can picture
what uneducated villagers think and say, and can reproduce on
paper the picture which imagination has suggested. The gift is so
special, the difficulty is so great, the success is so complete, that
4

the words of George Eliot come on us as a new revelation of what society in quiet English parishes really is and has been. How hard it is to draw the poor may easily be seen if we turn to the ordinary tales of country life that are written in such abundance by ladies. There the poor are always looked at from the point of view of the rich. They are so many subjects for experimenting on, for reclaiming, improving, being anxious about, and relieving. They have no existence apart from the presence of a curate and a district visitor. They live in order to take tracts and broth. This is a very natural, and in some degree a very proper view for the well-intentioned rich to take of the poor. It is right that those who have spiritual and temporal blessings should care for the souls and bodies of those around them. But the poor remain, during the process and in its description, as a distinct race. What they think of and do when they are not being improved and helped, remains a blank. Those, too, who are above the reach of occasional destitution are entirely omitted from these portraitures of village life. Every one is agreed that it would be impertinent to improve a man who gets anything like a pound a week. When, therefore, George Eliot describes the whole of a village, from the simple squire down to the wheelwright and his wife, the ground thus occupied is virgin soil.

There are two chapters in *Silas Marner* describing the conversation of a coterie at a public-house, and what they did and said on a man appearing before them to announce a robbery, which are perfectly wonderful. It is not, perhaps, saying much to say that an intelligent reader who knew beforehand that such a scene was to be described would be utterly puzzled to think of any one thing that such people could satisfactorily be represented as remarking or doing. But some notion of what George Eliot can do may be obtained by comparing what the best writers of the day are in the habit of doing when they attempt scenes of this sort. Sir Edward Lytton and Mr. Dickens would venture to try such a scene if it came in their way. Sir Edward Lytton would only go so far as to put some very marked character or some very important personage of the story in the centre of the group, and put everything into relation and connexion with him. This is really the good ladies' novel view of the poor in another shape. The poor cluster round some one superior to them, and the only reason of the superiority which Sir Edward Lytton can claim, so far as he can claim any at all, arises from the poor being supposed to be in a position of greater naturalness and simplicity. They are represented as taking their ease in their inn, and not as being talked to by their anxious-minded betters. Mr. Dickens sets himself to draw the poor and the uneducated much more thoroughly, but his mode is to invest each person with one distinguishing peculiarity. This gives a distinctness to each picture, but it makes the whole group artificial and mechanical. He always, or almost always, keeps us in the region of external peculiarities. We are made to notice the teeth, the hair, the noses, the buttons of the people described, or some oddity of manner that marks them. The sentiment of the poor is often caught in Mr. Dickens's works with great happiness, and the chance observations that they might make under particular circumstances are well conceived; but George Eliot goes far beyond this. The people in the public-house in *Silas Marner* proclaim in a few words each a distinct and probable character, and sustain it. The things they say are perfectly natural, and yet show at once what the sayers are like. We know that these poor are like real poor people, just as we know that the characters in Shakespeare are like real men and women. The humour of the author, of course, pervades the representation, just as it does in the comic parts of Shakespeare. Our enjoyment in a large measure depends on the enjoyment of the writer; nor is it probable that any group at a pothouse would really say so many things on any one evening that, if recorded, would amuse us so much. But this is one of the exigencies of art. In order not to waste space, that which is characteristic must be placed closely together. Were it not for this absence of dilution, the history of the village group of Raveloe, the village in which the scenes of *Silas Marner* are laid, might be a mere record of an actual evening passed at a country public. It is a kind of unpermissible audacity in England to say that anything is as good as Shakespeare, and we will not therefore say that this public-house scene is worthy of the hand that drew Falstaff and Poins; but we may safely say that, however much less in degree, the humour of George Eliot in such passages is of the same kind as that displayed in the comic passages of Shakespeare's historical plays.

There are two points especially with regard to the poor which George Eliot has mastered, and the mastery of which lends a lifelike reality to *Silas Marner*. These are the frankness of the poor and their religion. The villagers in *Silas Marner* speak out. They say what they have to say, and do not mince matters. This is the rudeness of persons who do not mean to be rude; for they do not dream of the rules which a consideration for the feelings of others teaches those who are more refined. When Silas Marner, the hero of the story, a poor weaver, loses his money, he is visited by a Job's comforter in the person of the parish clerk. This comforter comes in the dignity of a parish official and a parish wit, and with really kind intentions, to say a kind thing to a man whom he dislikes and despises, but yet respects a little, and pities a great deal. He explains to Silas that he has no call to 'sit a-moaning.' In old times he used to think that Silas was no better than he should be. 'You were allays a staring, white-faced creatur, partly like a bald-faced calf, as I may say.' The clerk's candour, however, prompted him to own that this may have been an unjust pre-possession. 'There's no knowing; it isn't every queer looksed thing as Old Harry's had the making of;' and he proceeds to explain that Silas may be compared to 'toads, and such,' which are often harmless, and useful against vermin. He ends by advising Silas to keep up his spirits, and by combating an objection that was more deeply felt by himself and by his companions than by the weaver. It had been supposed that Silas was a man of mystery and cunning, and burdened with a great secret. This notion the clerk rejected, and took an opportunity of at once showing his own wisdom and of patronising Silas, by informing him that he did not share this sombre view of the weaver's character. 'As for thinking you're a deep un, and ha' got more inside you nor 'ull bear day-light, I'm not o' that opinion at all, and so I tell the neighbours. For, says I, you talk o' Master Marner making out a tale, why it's nonsense, that is; it 'ud take a 'cute man to make a tale like that; and, says I, he looked as scared as a rabbit.'

This is only one specimen of the direct, and, as rich people would think, insulting language which George Eliot, with the happiest effects, puts into the mouth of the poor. But the author knows the class described too well to show them long together without the intervention of deep feeling of some sort. The Job's comforter is succeeded by a real comforter—by a motherly, patient, humble-minded woman. Dolly Winthrop, with her quaint kindness, her simple piety, and her good sense, is as touching and at the same time as amusing a character as George Eliot has drawn. She comes in with her little boy, and brings some cakes which she thinks will give a little pleasure to Silas in his affliction. 'There's letters pricked on 'em,' said Dolly. 'I can't read 'em myself, and there's nobody rightly knows what they mean; but they've a good meaning, for they're the same as is on the pulpit-cloth at church.' Silas explains what the letters are, on which Dolly replies that she has often been told before, but they slip out of her mind again; 'the more's the pity, for they're good letters, else they wouldn't be in the church; and so I prick 'em on all the loaves and all the cakes, though sometimes they wont hold, because o' the rising, for if there's any good to be got we've need on it i' this world, that we have.' Dolly subsequently tries to induce Silas to go to church on Christmas-day, which she says will be the best source of consolation he can have, as she herself has felt. 'If a bit o' trouble comes, I feel as I can put up wi' it, for I've looked for help i' the right quarter, and gev myself up to Them as we must all give ourselves up to at the last; and if we've done our part, it isn't to be believed as Them as are above us will be worse nor we are, and come short o' Theirn.' This simple Raveloe theology, as the author calls it, ultimately tells greatly on the weaver, although at first his comprehension was 'baffled by the plural pronoun, which was no heresy of Dolly's, but only her way of avoiding a presumptuous familiarity.' She did everything in her power to allure the weaver to church—made her little boy sing his carol, 'which he did with a clear chirp and in a melody that had the rhythm of an industrious hammer'—and told how the 'bassoon and voices,' and the Christmas music generally, make you think you've got to a better place already. And then her rustic piety is afraid that this implies a rather more unhandsome reflection on the present state of existence than is altogether warrantable. 'I wouldn't speak ill o' this world, seeing as Them put us in it that knows best; but what wi' the drink, and the quarrelling, and the bad illnesses, and the hard dying as I've seen times and times, one's thankful to hear of a better.' The difference, so far as truthfulness of description and insight into the poor go, between George Eliot and the usual lady-novelist, cannot be better estimated than by contrasting Dolly and her I.H.S. cakes, her reverent belief in 'Them,' and her views of this world and the next, with a model cottager's wife of domestic fiction. The one is a living woman, the other is an improveable puppet.

We wish to avoid telling the story of Silas Marner to those who have not read the book, and it fortunately happens that there is nothing in the story that calls for observation. There does not appear to us to be a fault in the plot or in the working of it out.

The errors that marred the *Mill on the Floss* have been entirely avoided. The classes which the author can draw, and those alone, have been drawn. There is nothing like the inanity of Stephen Guest or the spiritual conflicts of Maggie. On the other hand, the plot secures the writer from the danger of trespassing on unknown ground which was the origin of some weaknesses in *Adam Bede*. The trial and the reprieve of Hetty were incomparably the worst parts of the story, for the simple reason that the writer evidently knew nothing about trials and reprieves. There is, again, nothing painful in *Silas Marner*. The secret is one that it is not distressing either to have concealed or to find out, and the misery of those who are miserable is not of a very intense kind. We are left unembarrassed to enjoy those pictures of humble life which have constituted the great merit of George Eliot's works, and which appear in this new volume with as much freshness, novelty, and humour as ever. All that can be said against *Silas Marner*, as compared with its predecessors, is that it is shorter, and therefore slighter. The author has less ground to cover, and has not been obliged to fill up space with improbable incidents or painful scenes. The work has therefore been easier. The characters have had to be sustained for a shorter time, and the delineation of mental conflicts and emotions has been more in outline. If we take into consideration all the difficulties encountered and surmounted, *Adam Bede* still remains perhaps the author's greatest production. But, within its limits, *Silas Marner* is quite equal to either of its predecessors, and, in combining the display of the author's characteristic excellences with freedom from blemishes and defects, is perhaps superior.

❡ *Silas Marner* was well received: *The Westminster Review*, amid a great deal of wild praise, said that it was her best book yet. And on the whole, the book was praised for the qualities in it that we admire today: for the realism, the portrayal of the poor and middling among Raveloe society, and above all (perhaps) the magnificent scene at the Rainbow in chapter 6. *The Times*, in fact, was so delighted with the realism of the first part of the book, that it expressed a polite disappointment at the way the style changed to that of a fable: 'In two-thirds of the volume we have Silas Marner before us in his hopeless, helpless estrangement from his fellow men. The picture of his silent misery is filled in so carefully, the canvas is spread so large, and we are introduced to so many of his neighbours, that when, at the 240th page, we find the weaver of Raveloe adopting little Eppie as his own child we feel that the story is about to commence.' A pity, then, the reviewer went on, that the actual regeneration of Silas by Eppie is not shown us— that we jump to the time, sixteen years later, when he is already changed. 'The first part, forming more than two-thirds of the volume, is thus a magnificent portico to the second part, which is a pretty little cottage, hidden behind a mass of more stately architecture.' But he promptly added that he could not regard this objection seriously: and the rest of the long review consists of unqualified praise.

The one notice we have included, from *The Saturday Review*, makes much the same points as the others, but with a greater range of reference, and perhaps, occasionally, a greater perceptiveness. Praise of the 'unknown, and to most people unknowable, section of society' in which much of the story moves was common; but the comparison with Lytton and Dickens is peculiar to this critic, and opens for us a glimpse into Victorian attitudes towards the social novel. The praise of George Eliot's frankness ('the direct, and, as rich people would think, insulting language which George Eliot, with the happiest effects, puts into the mouth of the poor') is rather pedestrian, but in a spirit the author would surely have appreciated. The concluding remarks on her previous novels are interesting. We catch the almost inevitable Victorian fear of touching pitch when we read 'there is nothing painful in *Silas Marner*'; and no doubt it is this attitude which explains why the reviewer disliked the spiritual conflicts of Maggie Tulliver.

V · ROMOLA

❡ *Romola* was written during 1862 and the first half of 1863. It was serialised in the *Cornhill* magazine between July 1862 and the following August, and published in three volumes by Smith Elder and Co. on 6 July 1863. It was the only novel of George Eliot's not published by Blackwood's.

The Spectator, 18 July 1863

It was easy to be mistaken in the first chapters of this book, and it is pleasant to acknowledge that we were mistaken, and had not the insight to see the first faint signs of one of the greatest works of modern fiction. It is from no desire to vindicate that mistake that we regret that *Romola* should have been published in fragments. That it was not in any way affected by this mode of publication,—that it was not written in fragments, but was created by a continuous artistic effort, is clear enough. Still, perhaps, that is one reason for the inadequacy of the first impression. George Eliot's drawings all require a certain space, like Raffael's Cartoons, and are not of that kind which produce their effect by the reiteration of scenes each complete in itself. You have to unroll a large surface of the picture before even the smallest *unit* of its effect is attained. And this is far more true of this, probably the author's greatest work, than of her English tales. In the latter, the constant and striking delineation of social features with which we are all familiar, satisfies the mind in the detail almost as much as in the complete whole. It takes a considerable space to get a full view of Hetty or Dinah in 'Adam Bede,' and a still greater space to understand the characters of Adam, or of Arthur Donnithorne. But, in the meantime, the vivid detail, the dry humour, the English pictures with which we are all so familiar, fascinate and satisfy us even before we have gained this clear view of the whole characters. This cannot be so when even greater power is shown in mastering the life of a foreign nation in a past age. We do not care

about the light Florentine buzz with which so great a part of the
first volume is filled. Its allusions are half riddles, and its liveliness
a blank to us. Small local colours depend for their charm on the
familiarity of small local knowledge. Then, again, George Eliot is—
we will not say much greater as an imaginative painter of characters
than as an imaginative painter of action, for action, also, she paints
with marvellous power,—but much more inclined for the one than
the other. What her characters *do* is always subordinate with her
to what they *are*. This is the highest artistic power, but it carries its
inconveniences with it. She does not carry her readers *away*, as it
is called; it is generally easy to stop reading her; she satisfies you
for the moment, and does not make you look forward to the end.
She has Sir Walter Scott's art for revivifying the past,—but not
Scott's dynamical force in making you plunge into it with as
headlong an interest as into the present. For this she compensates
by a deeper and wider intellectual grasp,—but still it is easy enough
to understand why half-developed characters, sketched in with
unfamiliar local colours on a background of history that has long
melted away, should have looked strange and uninviting, especially
when not carried off by any exciting current of event, to the
ordinary reader's eye. It is marvellous that, in spite of these dis-
advantages, the wide and calm imaginative power of the writer
should have produced a work which is likely to be permanently
identified with English literature,—in which Italy and England
may feel a common pride.

The great artistic purpose of the story is to trace out the conflict
between liberal culture and the more passionate form of the
Christian faith in that strange era, which has so many points of
resemblance with the present, when the two in their most characteristic forms struggled for pre-eminence over Florentines who had
been educated into the half-pedantic and half-idealistic scholarship
of Lorenzo de Medici, who faintly shared the new scientific impulses
of the age of Columbus and Copernicus, and whose hearts and
consciences were stirred by the preaching, political as well as
spiritual, of one of the very greatest as well as earliest of the
reformers—the Dominican friar Savonarola. No period could be
found when mingling faith and culture effervesced with more
curious result. In some great and noble minds the new Learning,
clearing away the petty rubbish of Romanist superstition, and
revealing the mighty simplicities of the great age of Greece, grew
into a feeling that supplied all the stimulus of fever, if not the rest

of faith, and of these the author has drawn a very fine picture in the blind Florentine scholar, Romola's father, Bardo, who, with a restless fire in his heart, 'hung over the books and lived with the shadows' all his life. Nothing is more striking and masterly in the story than the subtle skill with which the dominant influence of this scholarship over the imagination of the elder generation of that time,—the generation which saw the first revival of learning, is delineated in the pictures of Bardo and Baldassarre. In the former you get something like a glimpse of the stately passion for learning which, in a later age (though England was then naturally behind Italy), took so vital a hold of the intellect of Milton, and overlaid his powerful imagination with all its rich fretwork of elaborate classical allusion. In the latter character,—Baldassarre, the same impression is conveyed in a still more subtle and striking form, because by painting the intermittent flashes of intellectual power in a scholar's failing memory, and its alternations with an almost animal passion of revenge, we gain not only a more distinct knowledge of the relative value in which scholarship was there and then held as compared with other human capacities, but a novel sense of sympathy which, in an age of diffused culture like this, it is not very easy to attain with the extravagance, as we should now think, of the price set upon it. There are few passages of subtler literary grandeur in English romance than that which paints the electrifying effect of a thrill of vindictive passion on Baldassarre's paralyzed memory, in recalling once more his full command of Greek learning, and the sense of power which thus returned to him:—

'He leaned to take up the fragments of the dagger; then he turned towards the book which lay open at his side. It was a fine large manuscript, an odd volume of Pausanias. The moonlight was upon it, and he could see the large letters at the head of the page:

ΜΕΣΣΗΝΙΚΑ. ΚΒ′.

In old days he had known Pausanias familiarly; yet an hour or two ago he had been looking hopelessly at that page, and it had suggested no more meaning to him than if the letters had been black weather-marks on a wall; but at this moment they were once more the magic signs that conjure up a world. That moonbeam falling on the letters had raised Messenia before him, and its struggle against the Spartan oppression. He snatched up the book, but the light was too pale for him to read further by. No matter: he knew that chapter; he read inwardly. He saw the stoning of the traitor Aristocrates—stoned by a whole people, who cast him out from their borders to lie unburied, and set up a pillar with verses upon it, telling how Time had brought home justice to the unjust. The words arose within him, and stirred innumerable vibrations of memory. He forgot that he was old: he could almost have shouted. The light was come again, mother of knowledge and joy! In that exultation his limbs recovered their strength: he started up with his broken dagger and book, and went out under the broad moonlight. It was a nipping frosty air, but Baldassarre could feel no chill—he only felt the glow of conscious power. He walked about and paused on all the open spots of that high ground, and looked down on the domed and towered city, sleeping darkly under its sleeping guardians, the mountains; on the pale gleam of the river; on the valley vanishing towards the peaks of snow; and felt himself master of them all. That sense of mental empire which belongs to us all in moments of exceptional clearness, was intensified for him by the long days and nights in which memory had been little more than the consciousness of something gone. That city, which had been a weary labyrinth, was material that he could subdue to his purposes now: his mind glanced through its affairs with flashing conjecture; he was once more a man who knew cities, whose sense of vision was instructed with large experience, and who felt the keen delight of holding all things in the grasp of language. Names! Images!—his mind rushed through its wealth without pausing, like one who enters on a great inheritance.'

This passage, taken with those which lead up to it, whether they refer to Bardo or Baldassarre, has the effect of reproducing one great feature in the age of the revival of learning with the finest effect—that sense of large *human* power which the mastery over a great ancient language, itself the key to a magnificent literature, gave, and which made scholarship then a *passion*, while with us it has almost relapsed into an antiquarian dryasdust pursuit. We realize again, in reading about Bardo and Baldassarre, how, for these times, the first sentence of St. John, 'In the beginning was the Word,' had regained all its force, to the exclusion, perhaps, of the further assertion that the Word was with God and was God. That sense of the great *power* of language, of which we have now so little, which, indeed, it is the tendency of the present day to depreciate, was in that day full of a new vigour, and to some extent contested with the mysteries of the Gospel the control of great men's souls. This is the picture which Romola makes so living for us. We find here the strife between the keen definite knowledge of the reviving Greek learning, and the turbid visionary mysticism of the reviving Dominican piety. We find a younger generation, represented by Romola, and Dino, and Tito, that has inherited this scholarship, and finds it wholly inadequate for its wants, looking upon that almost as dry bones which the older generation felt to be stimulating nourishment,—and either turning from it, like Dino, to the rapture of mystical asceticism, or using it, like Tito, as a useful sharp-edged tool in the battle of Florentine politics, or trying, like Romola, to turn it to its true purpose, viz., that of clarifying and sifting the false from the true elements in the great mysterious faith presented to her conscience by Savonarola. The pride of laborious farseeing scholarship, gazing with clear scornful eyes at the inarticulate convulsive ecstasies of faith— all the powers of language rebelling passionately, as it were, against the deep and fervent passions which transcend the containing powers of language, and boil over its edges, in religious, or even in the opposite animal raptures,—this is a picture wonderfully painted, and which produces all the more impression, that the minute vivid ripple of the light gossip of the Florentine market-place gives a ground tone to the book.

This fundamental conflict between the Greek scholarship and the mystical Christian faith which runs through the book, is made even more striking by the treacherous character of the man who represents the Greek culture cut adrift from all vestige of moral or religious faith. The fine gradations of social dissimulation, so characteristic of Florence in the Medicean era, ranging from the one politic insincerity of Savonarola, which raises so grand a struggle in his mind, down to the easy-sliding treachery of Tito, bring up before us in another shape the characteristic contrasts of the age between that earnest spirit which revived the old culture, because it was *truer* than the degraded current superstitions,— that pliant worldliness which adopted, and adapted itself to it, because it was an instrument of finer edge and wider utility,—and lastly, that fervent faith which despised it as substituting the study of a dead past for the great conflict of a living present. Tito's smooth dissimulation is all the more striking a picture, because it comes out as the natural fruit of a mind almost incapable of either strong conviction or strong personal fidelity, gliding about in an age when strong convictions were coming to the birth, and among a race barely redeemed from that spirit of political falsehood which was just going to be called Machiavellian by a proud sense of loyalty to personal and party ties. Tito is pictured, as the Greeks of that time perhaps deserved to be pictured, not as originally false, but as naturally pleasure-loving, and swerving aside before every unpleasant obstacle in the straight path, at the instance of a quick intelligence and a keen dislike both to personal collisions and to personal sacrifices. His character is, to use a mathematical term, the osculating curve which touches that of each of the others at the surface, and nowhere else—Savonarola's at the point of his external political policy, Romola's in her love of beauty and hatred of the turbid malarious exhalations of visionary excitement, and the scholarly enthusiasm of Bardo only in the apt classical knowledge, by no means in the ardour of his love for it. On Tito's very first entrance on to the stage, the Florentine artist of the story, Piero di Cosimo, is eager to paint him as a Sinon, not that there is treachery in his face, but that there is in it the softness and suppleness, and gliding ease of movement, and nimbleness of intellect, which, in a time of political passion, seem likely to lead to treachery, because, first, they qualify, both intellectually and morally, for the traitor's part, and, next, they serve to mask his play. From this first scene, when the fatal ease of the man's manner is first suggested, to the noble scene at the conclusion, in which he sounds, and sounds successfully, Savonarola's too eager statesmanship, with intent to betray him to the Duke of Milan and the Pope, you see Tito's character grow into the foulest treachery, simply from its consistent desire to compass every pleasant end which suggests itself to him as feasible, without openly facing, if he can help it, any one's severe displeasure. Nor is anything drawn more finely than the peculiar species of fear which is an essential part of this character,—a fear which, in the last resort, spurs the keen intellect of the man into a certain desperate energy, but which usually remains too cowardly even to understand itself, and lurks on in the character as a kind of unconscious resentment against those who wring from him the exercise of such an energy. A character essentially treacherous only because it is full of soft *fluid* selfishness is one of the most difficult to paint. But whether when locking up the crucifix, which Romola received from her dying brother's hands, in the little temple crowned with the figures of Ariadne and Bacchus, and fondly calling her 'Regina mia,' which somehow conveys that he less *loves* the woman than passionately admires her—or buying his 'garment of fear,' the coat of light chain armour, from the armour-smith,—or thoughtlessly deceiving the poor little contadina Tessa by the mock marriage at the carnival—or shrinking before Romola's indignation into that frigid tone of empty affectionateness which is the clearest sign of a contracted heart—or interpreting the Latin proclamation to the people with a veil of good-nature over his treacherous purpose—or crowned in the feast at the Rucellai Gardens, and paling suddenly beneath Baldassarre's vindictive glance—or petting Tessa and her children in his hiding-place on the hill—the same wonderful power is maintained throughout, of stamping on our imagination with the full force of a master hand a character which seems naturally too fluent for the artist's purpose. There is not a more wonderful piece of painting in English romance than this figure of Tito.

Of Romola it is less easy to say whether one is absolutely satisfied or not. The soupçon of hardness of which one is conscious as somewhat detracting from her power, the skill with which the author has prepared us for a mental struggle exactly similar, even in its minutest features, to what might occur today between the claims of a sublime faith appealing to the conscience, and a distaste for miracle or vision in its prophet, the striking contrast with Tessa, the ignorant 'pretty little pigeon,' who thinks every one who is kind to her a saint,—all render it a little difficult to say whether we know her intimately, or whether we have only a very artistic idea of what she is *not*, and what she *is* only by inference and contrast. Our own feeling is that Romola is the least perfect figure in the book, though a fine one,—that she is a shade more modernized than the others, several shades less individual, and, after all, though the pivot of her character turns, as it were, on faith, that she does not distinctly show any faith except the faith in rigid honour, in human pity, and partially also in Savonarola's personal greatness and power. We do not say the character is not natural,— we only say it is half-revealed and more suggested than fully painted, though these harder feminine characters always seem to ask to be outlined more strongly than any others.

But the great and concentrated interest of the book—at least, after the wonderful development of Tito's character—is the portrait of Savonarola, which it is almost impossible not to feel as faithful as history, as it is great as romance. You see the same large human-

hearted Italian Luther, narrower than Luther on some sides,
owing to the thin Medicean culture against which he led the reaction, but with a far more statesmanlike and political purpose, and
far more fiery imagination, the same, in fact, whom Mr. Maurice
has delineated intellectually with so much delicate fidelity in his
history of modern philosophy, and who impresses himself upon us
in almost everything he wrote, but yet never before presented
clearly to the eye. His portrait evinces almost as great a graphic
power, and far more scrupulous care than Sir Walter Scott used
in those pictures of the various Stewarts which will certainly outlive
the very different originals. Nothing can be finer and more impressive—nothing more difficult to make fine and impressive—than
Savonarola's exhortation to Romola to return to the home from
which she was flying. You see in every word the man's profound
trust in God as the author of all human ties, and of all social and
political ties, breaking through the fetters of his Dominican order,
and asserting the divine order *in* nature rather than the divine
order *out of* nature. This, however, is not the finest picture given
of him. The finest is contained in the profoundly pathetic scene in
which Savonarola, having in the fervour of his eloquence committed God to working him a miracle at the right moment, is
brought to book both by his enemies and friends on the question
of the trial by fire, and kneels in prayer that in fact refuses to be
prayer, but rises into a political debate within himself as to the
policy of seeming to take a step which he knows he must somehow
evade. 'While his lips were uttering audible *cor mundum crea in me*,
his mind was still filled with the images of the snare his enemies
had prepared for him, still busy with the arguments by which he
could justify himself against their taunts and accusations.' But
the scene is too long and too fine for us to spoil it by snatching it
from the context, and is, indeed, closely bound up with the noble
picture of the encounter with Tito which follows. Our author
rejects apparently the authenticity of the last great words attributed to Savonarola as he is dying on the scaffold, which Mr.
Maurice accepts. 'The voice of the Papal emissary,' says the
historian of philosophy, 'was heard proclaiming that Savonarola
was cut off from the Church militant and triumphant. Another
voice was heard saying, "No, not from the Church triumphant,
they cannot shut me out of that."' It is a pity that George Eliot
rejects, as we suppose she does, the evidence for these words. They
would have formed a far higher artistic ending to her story than

the somewhat feeble and womanish chapter with which it con-
cludes,—the only blot on the book. Large and genial as is the
sympathy with Savonarola, there is, perhaps, no wish to represent
his faith altogether as a triumphant faith. Yet Romola's faith in
goodness and self-sacrifice, and in little children and 'the eternal
marriage of love and duty,' and so forth, which the proem tells us
is ever to last, would be an idle dream for the world, without a
Christ in whose eternal nature all these realities live and grow.

But the defects, if they are defects, in this book, and the certainly
somewhat unfortunate amplification of Florentine gossip in the
first volume, before the reader is drawn into that rushing tide of
Savonarola's revolution round the skirts of which Tito's treacherous destiny hovers, like a bird of prey over a raging battle,
are blemishes too slight to do more than distinguish still more
vividly the high purpose and calm imaginative serenity of this
great romance. It will never be George Eliot's most popular book,—
it seems to us, however, much the greatest she has yet produced.

[?R. H. HUTTON]

❡ Most readers today (especially those who have not read it)
assume that *Romola* is the worst of George Eliot's novels. There is a
feeling that by setting the story in fifteenth-century Florence,
George Eliot hung chains round her own powers. Determined to
have in this book too the realistic dialogue, the feel of daily life,
that are so powerful in her English stories, she is forced to build
them up from her reading instead of her memory. The result is a
forced spontaneity, an academic recreation of what in the other
novels is immediate and genuine.

All this is true. It may not be such a serious fault as is often
assumed (the everyday life of Florence is not the centre of the
book's interest); and it is perhaps an objection to historical novels
in general, not merely to *Romola*. Still, it is an objection, and a
widely agreed one today. Was it felt at the time?

It is not easy to be certain of this. More than one reviewer thought
that *Romola* was her masterpiece. *The Westminster Review* wrote:
'It cannot be denied that *Romola* is less popular than its predecessors, but we do not hesitate to say that it is its author's
greatest work'; and *The Spectator* (whose review we have chosen

for inclusion) called it 'one of the greatest works of modern fiction'. Others, however, were politely disappointed at the change to a historical setting: '. . . It seems a pity that these things should be done by the authoress of *Adam Bede*. A lesser hand might have been employed to collect these simple treasures. However instructive it may be, it is not without a tax on our patience that we read long accounts of Florentine antiquities, and translations of sermons by Savonarola, and extracts from chronicles of processions . . .' (*The Saturday Review*, 25 July 1863.)

And more may have thought this than said it: for when *Felix Holt* appeared, there was something like a sigh of relief that she had returned to an English setting. The *Edinburgh Review* waited until *Felix Holt* before delivering itself of what seems a strong irritation with *Romola*: 'One sentence of Tommy Trounsem's in *Felix Holt* is well worth all the pages which are allotted to the Florentine Figaro.' The basis of the *Edinburgh's* irritation (or is this just careless wording?) was not merely the antiquarianism but also the accuracy of the historical treatment: 'The novelist and poet ought to speak out of the fulness of the heart, as George Eliot reveals without effort the odd mysteries of custom and character which grow up in some remote Midland village. The exquisite inaccuracy of Shakespeare and of Scott belongs to the essence of historical fiction.' (*The Edinburgh Review*, October 1866.)

The Westminster Review used similar strictures, but confined them to 'the mass of readers', and thought the antiquarianism less an intrinsic blemish than a bar to popularity: 'No! *Romola* is not likely to be generally popular; it is too great both in mind and heart.' The one direct criticism this reviewer made of the historical setting was rather a shrewd one. After pointing out that George Eliot's interest in the events of her story was negligible compared with her interest in the effects these events had on the character of Tito, he laments that this has made her rather cavalier in her use of coincidence. The Florentine setting, with its air of remoteness (and therefore of unlikely events being possible) may, he suggests, have made this worse.

We have included the *Spectator* review, an enthusiastic and intelligent defence of the whole book, including the history. Hutton has seen that the 'stately passion for learning' is the one thing that spoke direct from the fifteenth century to George Eliot's own imagination; and he is surely right in seizing on Baldassare's return of memory in chapter 38 ('The Black Marks become Magical') as the most moving rendering of this. Turning to the individual characters, this reviewer sees (like most readers, then and now) that its finest achievement is Tito, that typical George Eliot figure whose aversion to any unpleasantness slowly corrupts his charm into a total egoism: a profounder and crueller version of what she had sketched in Arthur Donnithorne. Perhaps the comments on Savonarola are more indulgent than we would now endorse, but time has not soured any of the other praise.

VI · FELIX HOLT

⟪ *Felix Holt* was written between March 1865 and the following May, and published on 15 June 1866.

The Saturday Review, 16 June 1866

. . . The popular notion about the excellence and brilliancy of the style of George Eliot's novels is that it is simply the excellence of a painter like Teniers. People talk of *Silas Marner* as if there were nothing in it except Nancy Lammeter and the famous meeting in the parlour of the inn; of the *Mill on the Floss*, as if it were only a rural chronicle of Gleggs and Dodsons and Tullivers; of *Adam Bede*, as if it contained no more than a photographic reproduction of the life of midland dairies and farm-houses and apple-orchards. No doubt the same kind of remarks will be made about the latest, and in some points the best, of the writer's stories. And there is no lack of material even for the limited appreciation involved in such criticism as this. The talk of the miners over their ale; of the respectable farmers and shopkeepers over their three-and-sixpenny ordinary in the country market-town; of the upper servants in the butler's pantry of an old manor-house, is as witty and as truthful, and in its own way as artistically admirable, as anything that the writer has ever done. And the variety is much greater among these quaint-speaking souls, with narrow slow-moving lives, and only the dimmest and haziest outlook, and the most heavily-clogged sensibilities. Instead of the one or two who have hitherto sufficed to furnish a background for the graver and more tragic action of the story, in *Felix Holt* there are a dozen. There is the Dissenting minister's old servant who is always being severely 'exercised' in spirit, who, if remonstrated with for boiling the eggs too hard, would sigh that 'there's hearts as are harder,' and who, in reply to anything like a joke, would exclaim, 'Dear me, don't you be so light, Miss; we may all be dead before night;' and the good-humoured pitman who says that he's 'been aforced to give

my wife a black eye to hinder her from going to the preachin';
Lors-a-massy, she thinks she knows better nor me.' There is the
little old waiting-woman who looks on life as she looks on her
evening game of whist, 'I don't enjoy the game much, but I like
to play my cards well, and see what will be the end of it.' And there
is Mrs. Holt, the groaning member of the church assembled in
Malthouse Yard, who, though full of humble professions, avows,
'I've done *my* duty and more if anybody comes to that; for I've
gone without my bit of meat to make broth for a sick neighbour;
and if there's any of the church members say they've done the
same, I'd ask them if they had the sinking at the stomach as I
have.' These are only three or four out of a much greater number
of similar characters, all fully and clearly drawn, and each
thoroughly different from the other, except in the one point of
leading a dull uncultured life. For though they all say good things,
what they say is not all good in the same way, but because it is in
each case the natural style of a distinct character which has been
keenly observed and fully conceived. . . .

One of these puzzles, which runs pathetically through *Felix Holt*
as through *Romola* and the *Mill on the Floss*, is the evil usage which
women receive at the hands of men. Mrs. Transome, in the novel
before us, is perhaps a stronger illustration than either Maggie
Tulliver or Romola of the curse which a man can be to a woman.
And it is not designed for a mere outburst of impotent anger and
misery when she exclaims, partly crushed, partly defiant, that
'God was cruel when he made women.' She gives a reason for her
seemingly impious accusation, and her own history and position
supplied an extenuating condition, or else an argument in its
support. 'A woman's love,' she said, 'is always freezing into fear;
she wants everything, she is secure of nothing. . . . What is the
use of a woman's will? if she tries, she doesn't get it, and she
ceases to be loved.' Fate had been unkind to the unhappy woman.
'After sharing the common dream that when a beautiful man-child
was born to her, her cup of happiness would be full, she had
travelled through long years apart from that child to find herself
at last in the presence of a son of whom she was afraid, and to
whose sentiment in any given case she possessed no key.' This is a
picture of which men would have seen more, and thought more, if
they had been less ready to avoid pitying women in the right place
by a willingness to pity them in the wrong place, where they don't
either merit or want pity. Mrs. Transome has other causes than a

rather cold and self-reliant son to exclaim, 'I would not lose the misery of being a woman, now I see what can be the baseness of a man.' 'One must be a man—first to tell a woman that her love has made her your debtor, and then ask her to pay you by breaking the last poor threads between her and her son.' The whole chapter descriptive of the interview in which a man tries to save himself from disagreeable things by inducing a woman whom he has once loved to confess her past degradation to her own son, is a painful though unsurpassedly vigorous delineation of the ugliness to which anybody can stoop when 'led on through years by the gradual demands of a selfishness which has spread its fibres far and wide through the intricate vanities and sordid cares of an everyday existence.' This is the old strain of *Romola* taken up again. Mr. Jermyn, like Tito, is guilty of a hateful baseness, not because he is a wicked ravening fiend, but because he is weak and mean, and has got to think honour and pity and affection and every other virtue in his relations to another cheaply sacrificed at the price of some gain to himself. 'To such uses may tender relations come when they have ceased to be tender.'

Yet this strong and repeated conviction of how hard or mean or cruel men are to women has not prevented the authoress, here as in other books, from making a man the effective stirrer-up of a pure and lofty enthusiasm in the mind of her heroine. What Savonarola was to Romola, Felix Holt is to Esther. Only the first had the simpler and stronger lever of religion, while Felix Holt elevates Esther to a height as lofty as his own by the subtle force of his own character. It need scarcely be said that the task which the authoress has set herself in the later case is by much the more difficult, and demands a new delicacy and ingenuity. Religious enthusiasm is full of infection, and might have easily grown up under the teaching of Savonarola in a much less noble and less bitterly tried person than Romola was. But enthusiasm for a teacher who brings no pietistic exaltation to his work, and only preaches the doctrine of self-denial from the social point of view and in its least attractive shape, implies a curious and subtle affinity between the teacher and the proselyte. This affinity and its development are very finely brought out. In the mind of a rather dainty heroine, whose taste for the minor graces of life was revolted by ugly and dull surroundings, the growth of an appreciation for the mental elevation and robustness which are so much above the minor graces is traced with a singularly supple force. And the study was well worth making, of the impression produced by a robust, self-reliant, undevout, yet thoroughly noble character upon a mind into none of whose moods the doctrines of Calvinistic theology happened to fit. It is a study which suits a time when even the Carlylian gospel of labour, greatly as it needs to be modified for much good to come of it, has done something for people who found that nothing was done for them by formulas about Predestination and Grace and Faith. But in *Felix Holt* the most elevated form of what may without offence be called modern paganism makes way where a dull cut-and-dried theology was worthless, because it was embodied in a vehement and enthusiastic man, who does not shrink from even throwing away a livelihood which he thought involved a trick upon his fellows. The suppleness with which Esther is developed is more than matched in the strong-handed consistency with which the authoress has drawn her hero. It is a pity that the plot of the story, which runs upon the gradual disclosure of a claim to some property, happens to flow from utterly remote and far-off incidents, instead of flowing from the mental movement of the principal actors. Until Esther is taken away in her carriage by Mrs. Transome, the movement of the plot and the movement of character rather jar and clang together. It is true that in the end the possible possession of the property becomes a hinge in the play of character, but meanwhile it has thrown a considerable artificialness over portions of the story. This, however, is only a slight drawback in what is essentially a novel of character, and the figure of Felix Holt stands out with such size and strength, and almost incisive freshness, as to overshadow any minor defect of construction. Behind him there are the other two most conspicuous persons in the book—the sorrowful woman, whose life has been robbed of all its savour and with a terrible secret crushing her heart, and, in effective relief with her, the gentle, ripe-minded, fervent old Dissenting minister, whose views about salvation were barely high enough to please his flock. The authoress's creative energy has never, we think, been so exuberantly exercised before. One group succeeds another, and not a single figure appears in any of them, though it be ever so far in the background, which is not perfectly drawn and perfectly coloured. Even the young ladies at the Manor, who only ask when Dissent began, why Government didn't put a stop to it, and so on, illustrate the intense finish which this accomplished and profound writer puts on every part of her work. Of her exquisite humour, her subtlety and delicacy of analysis, the wide suggestiveness of her bits of 'aside,' and her style which is so fascinating because it is so exact an outward expression of the deep and mellow power with which her mind works and by which it is coloured—of all these we need not speak. They are as perfect and as delightful as they ever were.

The Times, 26 June 1866

Hitherto Miss Austen has had the honour of the first place among our lady novelists, but a greater than she has now arisen—a lady who in grasp of thought, in loftiness of feeling, in subtlety of expression, in fineness of humour, in reach of passion, and in all those sympathies which go to form the true artist has never been excelled. In the art of weaving a narrative Miss Austen is still pre-eminent among women. Nothing can be more natural than the way in which she evolves an event, leading up to it with the clearest motives and the most likely accidents, never saying too much, never too little, nothing too soon, nothing to late; sparing of reflection, and letting her characters speak for themselves. George Eliot has not attained this ease of story-telling because she has to deal with subjects far more difficult than Miss Austen ever attempted, with wilder passions, with stronger situations, with higher thoughts. Miss Austen scarcely ever gets out of the humdrum of easy-going respectable life; she can therefore well afford to be calm and neat in arranging every thread of the narrative she has to weave. George Eliot undertakes to set forth the issues of a more tumultuous life, to work out deeper problems, and to play with torrents where Miss Austen played with rills. But if thus dealing with stronger forces she has been as a rule unable to give to her plots the finished ease of movement for which her predecessor is famous, she on the other hand succeeds in veiling any deficiency of story by the wondrous charm of her style. We don't know any Englishwoman who can be placed near her as a writer of prose. There is such a pith in her thinking, such a charm in her writing, such a fresh vigour in the combination of both, that—begin where we will in her volumes—we go on reading, now startled by some strange suggestive thought, now tickled by her humour, now touched by her pathos, and ever fascinated by the results of delicate observation and fine literary polish. Her style is very rich, and not only rich with the palpable meaning which in each individual sentence she has to express, but rich also in those swift, indescribable associations which well chosen words recall, allusions to past reading, the reflected sparkle of past thinking, the fragrance of past feeling.

But, great as the charm of her style is, it is not her most attractive quality. Style will go far to cloak the deficiencies of a story, but it will not account for the strong interest which 'George Eliot' always contrives to awaken. The secret of her power is to be found in the depth and the range of her sympathies. She gets to the heart of her characters, and makes us feel with them, care for them, like to know about them. Even if they are stupid people who lead dull lives, she has the happy art of making us take an interest in their story and wish to hear it out. When we come to care for people—men or women—it really does not much matter what their story is: it fixes our attention. And for the most part we care or don't care for people according as we understand them or not. Dugald Stewart somewhere makes a rather suggestive remark to the effect that many of us are supposed to be wanting in benevolence when we are only wanting in attention or in imagination. The cruelties which we inflict on each other and our indifference to each other's sufferings are the result not of a cruel disposition, but of blindness and thoughtlessness and incapacity of imagination. And so it comes to pass that in most cases, if we can only be made to see people as they are, we learn to care for them. 'Seeing,' says the proverb, 'is believing;' but seeing also is feeling. And this is George Eliot's great gift that she sees and makes her readers see the personages of her tale; and we cannot truly see them, with all the stern conflict of their lives and with all the skeletons which they keep in their closets, without sharing in their hopes and fears, mixing in their griefs, and tasting of their joys. Be the man ever so dull, we become part of him and have a personal interest in his story the moment we can see him and understand him as George Eliot enables us to do. Great is Miss Austen's art of weaving a plot, and great is George Eliot's charm of style; but grandest of all as a means of exciting interest is that sympathy which sets a living character before us, and enables us not merely to see it, but also to feel it. . . .   [E. S. DALLAS]

The Nation (N.Y.), 16 August 1866

. . . As a novel with a hero there is no doubt that it *is* a failure. Felix is a fragment. We find him a Radical and we leave him what?

—only 'utterly married'; which is all very well in its place, but which by itself makes no conclusion. He tells his mistress at the outset that he was 'converted by six weeks' debauchery.' These very dramatic antecedents demanded somehow a group of consequents equally dramatic. But that quality of discretion which we have mentioned as belonging to the author, that tendency to avoid extreme deductions which has in some way muffled the crisis in each of her novels, and which, reflected in her style, always mitigates the generosity of her eloquence—these things appear to have shackled the freedom of her hand in drawing a figure which she wished and yet feared to make consistently heroic. It is not that Felix acts at variance with his high principles, but that, considering their importance, he and his principles play so brief a part and are so often absent from the scene. He is distinguished for his excellent good sense. He is uncompromising yet moderate, eager yet patient, earnest yet unimpassioned. He is indeed a thorough young Englishman, and, in spite of his sincerity, his integrity, his intelligence, and his broad shoulders, there is nothing in his figure to *thrill* the reader. . . .   HENRY JAMES

(Reprinted in *Notes & Reviews*, 1921)

❡ Perhaps no previous novel of George Eliot had so complex and interesting a reception as *Felix Holt*. Since the book contains (as all the reviewers pointed out and some complained) two almost distinct stories, it will be most convenient to consider the reactions to these separately.

The Transome story is certainly the greater: is there anything in George Eliot finer than the terribly lucid portrayal of Mrs Transome, old and hard, contemplating her empty life, speaking bitterly to the maid who is devoted to her (and whose life is by so much less empty), rebuking her former lover? All critics agree on this today, but not all did at the time. *The Spectator* singled out Harold Transome as 'the most original character in the book' and 'one of the most brilliant our author has ever drawn'; *The Saturday Review* (above) was impressed with Mrs Transome as an illustration 'of the curse which a man can be to a woman'. But the *Edinburgh*, at the other extreme, complained that 'an early intrigue between Mrs Transome and Mr Jermyn introduces a gratuitous and disagreeable complication'. The Transome story in fact was disliked by many: by those who disliked the 'disagreeable' strain in George Eliot, who considered her too outspoken, even cynical, in her treatment of human relations. Even *Blackwood's Magazine*, which (naturally enough) found it impossible not to praise everything she wrote, was less enthusiastic over this part of the book than over the story of Felix and Esther. This dislike of the disagreeable had all the disabling effects of prejudice; it caused the *Edinburgh* to dismiss as 'equally purposeless and painful' the final scene between Harold and Jermyn at the White Hart, which is surely one of the supreme dramatic encounters in English fiction.

The story of Felix himself is largely political in its interest and— as so often happens—we can guess the critic's political opinions from his response to the story. George Eliot was a radical in opinion, a conservative by temperament, and her ambivalent attitude is perfectly reflected in *Felix Holt*. Felix wishes to be 'A Radical—yes; but I want to go to some roots a good deal lower down than the franchise.' An unkind critic could point out that the effect of this is that Felix shows little interest in any of the actual items in the radical programme, and says hardly anything that would disturb the staunchest conservative. (He might point it out, but he would find that George Eliot had anticipated him, by telling us that Felix's speech on nomination day was applauded only by a few Tory bystanders.) When George Eliot set out her own political creed in 'Address to Working Men, by Felix Holt', which appeared in *Blackwood's Magazine* just after the second Reform Act, she told the working men that the possession of the franchise was worth nothing in itself; that 'the first thing we had better think of is, our heavy responsibility'; that great changes would not come 'in a hurry, by mere inconsiderable sweeping'; and she praised 'all the wonderful slow-growing system of things made up of our laws, our commerce, and our stores of all sorts'.

This vein of conservatism, this lack of real *political* radicalism, was spotted (usually with approbation or relief) by several reviewers. Thus *Blackwood's*: 'We are little likely, in this our grand climacteric (for Maga has just reached that interesting age) to adopt Radicalism of any shade; but if we ever see reason to change our political colours, we shall certainly follow Felix Holt rather

than John Bright.' (*Blackwood's Magazine,* July 1866.) And in its
obituary notice on George Eliot, Maga's critic wrote, in the same
strain: 'In January 1868 she contributed a pithy paper called an
"Address to Working-Men by Felix Holt" in which much sensible
advice was given to the operative classes who had been recently
enfranchised by the Reform Bill. From this paper, probably
better than from any other portion of her writings, a definite idea
of George Eliot's political sentiments may be gathered; and they
are such as neither Liberal nor Conservative will feel disposed to
quarrel with.' (*Blackwood's Magazine,* February 1881.) And the
radical *Westminster Review* made the point in reverse: complaining
that George Eliot had not given us any representation of the dark
social background that made men into radicals, and had therefore
painted the established order of society more favourably than it
deserved.

Yet Felix is a radical in sympathy. He is a man of the people (as
Harold Transome is not), and when he is angry with his fellow
workmen, it is with an anger privileged by the betrayed disappointment of one who is emotionally identified with them. It
is thus appropriate that he should insist on remaining a workman,
or should join in the election riot to try and steer it away from
harm. These democratic instincts were too much for some reviewers,
even for the *Westminster,* which wondered 'How far is he right in
his deliberate choice of poverty?' and went on in a fine strain of
bourgeois muddle: 'At the present day there is no need to discuss
the value of the text "the love of money is the root of all evil".
George Eliot must mean her words to be taken, like many of the
sayings in Plato's *Republic,* in a high allegorical sense. If they are
meant in any other they are simply mischievous.' (*Westminster
Review,* July 1866).

Felix's conduct in the riot came in for even more censure. 'He
is more fortunate than he deserves in obtaining a pardon,' said the
Edinburgh; his behaviour 'is simply that of a lunatic', said the
Westminster. Neither, however, explained what Felix should have
done—except, perhaps, follow the good conservative practice of
doing nothing.

And the character of Felix? Henry James is shrewd here, and
makes the now common complaint that 'there is nothing in his

figure to thrill the reader'. But surprisingly few reviewers found this; most of them assumed that because he was the central figure he was also the most successful. *The Saturday Review* is typical in saying that 'the figure of Felix Holt stands out with such size and strength, and almost incisive freshness, as to overshadow any minor defect of construction'. The point made just before this, by the same reviewer, seems not to have caught the attention of anyone else, but it is a good one. Felix Holt does correspond with Savonarola, and does differ from him in exerting his influence through the power of personality (and the fact that Esther is in love with him), without the additional strength of religious enthusiasm. For once we have a critic who can describe this 'modern paganism' without prejudice or irritation, even without disapproval.

One conclusion seems to emerge from all these reviews. *Felix Holt* aroused the prejudices of reviewers in a way *Romola* had not done, and the reaction to it was therefore less balanced. Almost everyone saw that Tito was the best thing in *Romola*; but political prejudice blinded some reviewers to the weaknesses of the Felix story, and moral prejudice blinded others (or even the same ones) to the excellences of the Transome story.

VII · MIDDLEMARCH

❡ On 7 May 1871 G. H. Lewes wrote to Blackwood that since his wife's new novel would need four volumes instead of three, and since 'you have more than once spoken of the desirability of inventing some mode of circumventing the Libraries and making the public *buy* instead of borrowing', it should be published in half-volume parts at intervals of one or two months. This was done, and *Middlemarch* came out in eight five-shilling parts, the first in November 1871, when it was not yet half-written (it was begun in December 1870, and finished in September 1872). The remaining parts followed in February, April, June, August, October, November and December. They were bound into four volumes and published at two guineas in December, and a guinea edition followed in February 1873.

Since the publication of *Middlemarch* was prolonged in this way, so was the reviewing. Many of the leading papers reviewed each part as it came out, and some of these notices are quite as interesting as those of the whole book.

Letter from John Blackwood, 9 October 1871

Strathtyrum / St. Andrews / N.B.
October 9/71

My Dear Lewes

Give my best regards to Mrs. Lewes and tell her that she who can administer to the world such glorious Tonics as Middlemarch must speedily cure herself of all ailments.

I put off the rereading in Type with a sort of 'slow reluctant' loving delay (which I daresay you well understand) until yesterday when my wife, not being 'too religious for family comfort,' having accepted my apologies for not accompanying her to Church, I sat down to the proof.

It transcends even my recollections of the first perusal in M.S.

and I passed the greater part of the day reading grinning and thinking as I read. Our scheme should succeed as this first part took me as much time to read as I would devote to many a large volume. I found myself pausing upon nearly every page to laugh and think over something equally happy in thought and expression. There is a perfect wealth of thought and fun and then it is real life. When I was transferred to the Vincy breakfast room I almost exclaimed aloud 'By Jove she is equally at home here.'

If I might venture a doubt about anything it is Mr. Casaubon's letter proposing. It is exceedingly funny but I mean is it not too transparently so not to strike even a girl so devoted to wisdom as poor dear Dodo. . . .

The Daily News, 28 November 1871

. . . At the very outset we are presented with a prelude which can only be described as an introductory air, written in a minor key, which is inexpressibly beautiful, and a trifle sad in tone; and here we gain our first conception of the heroine of the story, as she exists in the imagination of the author. In this prelude Miss Brooke is Saint Theresa, a woman of passionate idealisms, who longs to devote her life to noble aims, and is filled with indistinct yearnings after heroic action. Perhaps, we are told, this modern Theresa may find for herself no epic life, wherein there is 'a constant unfolding of far-resonant action;' but even in a Saint Theresa, who is 'foundress of nothing, whose loving heart-beats and sobs after an unattained goodness tremble off and are dispersed among hindrances, instead of centering in some long-recognizable deed,' there is a fine conception dear to the poetic heart. But in the Miss Brooke who actually figures in these pages there is a discordance. That strange insight which compels a man or woman of genius to tell the truth in spite of preconceived ideals leads George Eliot to treat Miss Brooke's fond aspirations with what looks to the reader painfully like sly and yet half sympathetic sarcasm. . . .

The Spectator, 1 June 1872

"The Melancholy of 'Middlemarch'"

We all grumble at 'Middlemarch;' we all say that the action is slow, that there is too much parade of scientific and especially physiological knowledge in it, that there are turns of phrase which are even pedantic, and that occasionally the bitterness of the commentary on life is almost cynical; but we all read it, and all feel that there is nothing to compare with it appearing at the present moment in the way of English literature, and not a few of us calculate whether we shall get the August number before we go for our autumn holiday, or whether we shall have to wait for it till we return. And yet does it really add to the happiness of its readers or not? We feel that we cannot do without it, that the criticisms on life given by our great novelist, and the pictures of life given by our great critic, are criticisms and pictures such as acquire a double value from the very fact that the criticisms are tested by such an insight and imagination as hers and the pictures criticised by a judgment so fine and balanced as hers;—but we question whether any one lays the book down without either an extra tinge of melancholy in his feeling, or in its place, a combative disposition to challenge the tendency and dispute the fidelity of tone of the pictures he has been studying. It is not in any degree true that the incidents are specially melancholy. On the contrary, the story is not at all of a gloomy description, and there are characters in it which the reader enjoys as he enjoys a gleam of warm sunshine on a dull October day,—especially that of Caleb Garth, the happy, eager, unworldly land-surveyor. Then, again there are pictures showing a humour so large and delicate that that laughter which really brightens the spirits breaks out even if we are alone,—especially the picture of the slip-shod-minded bachelor landowner, Mr. Brooke, with his weakness for an economical administration of his estate, his odds and ends of ideas, his desultory 'documents' on all sorts of subjects of which he hopes to see something effective made some day, his disposition to dabble in Liberalism, his easy-going, easily daunted ambition, and his indolent restlessness. Mr. Brooke, and Mrs. Cadwallader,—the crisp-minded, witty, worldly, aristocratic rector's wife,—are enough to cheer the reader of any story, however intellectual, even if we were not always coming in for whiffs of dry humour from other quarters,—from the genial, dubious-minded, whist-playing vicar, for instance, as well as from what George Eliot insists on calling the 'low people' of the story. Still, in spite of these snatches of warm sunshine, and of the frequent springs of delightful humour,— at the end of almost every part and every chapter, if not nearly every page, there comes an involuntary sigh. George Eliot never makes the world worse than it is, but she makes it a shade darker.

She paints the confusions of life no worse than they are, but she steadily discourages the hope that there is any light for us behind the cloud. She is large in her justice to the visible elements in human nature, but she throws cold water with a most determined hand on the idealism, as she evidently thinks it, which interprets by faith what cannot be interpreted by sympathy and sight.

For instance, in this new June part,—the ablest yet issued,— nothing can be more melancholy than the language of her final criticism on old Featherstone, not so much for its implied belief that there are plenty of human beings without any good at all left in them, as for the hint she throws out that it is those with the truest and deepest knowledge of man such as she and men of equal endowments possess, who have most reason to believe this, while the opposite belief,—the belief in 'the soul of goodness in things evil,'—is due to the idealism of merely theoretic opinion. 'If any one will here contend,' she says, 'that there must have been traits of goodness in old Featherstone, I will not presume to deny this; but I must observe that goodness is of a modest nature, easily discouraged, and when much elbowed in early life by unabashed vices, is apt to retire into extreme privacy, so that it is more easily believed in by those who construct a selfish old gentleman theoretically, than by those who form the narrower judgments based on his personal acquaintance.' The sneer there against the idealists increases instead of diminishing the melancholy impression produced. It seems to say not merely that the truest insight sees much more of unalloyed evil in the world than the sentimentalism of the day chooses to suppose, but that, after all, it does not very much matter,—that a sarcasm is quite as suitable, by way of attack on such a popular sentimentalism, as a grave and reluctant refutation. From George Eliot such a tone really jars us. Let her say, if she will, what no one has a better right to say with authority, that there are many characters so selfish as not to show a trace of anything good; but she should hardly say it with the taunting air of one who despises the world for its credulity.

Perhaps, however, the deepest symptom of melancholy in this book is the disposition so marked in it to draw the most reflective and most spiritual characters as the least happy. It is not a new thing for George Eliot to draw clergymen of large, tolerant, charitable character, with no great belief in dogma, and not a little secret uneasiness as to their position as spiritual teachers; but she always takes care that the larger the nature and the more spiritual the charity, the less is there any appearance of real rest and satisfaction of spirit. There are two clergymen of this class in 'Middlemarch,' Mr. Cadwallader, and Mr. Farebrother, both of them men of large nature and good hearts, but Mr. Farebrother certainly the abler and wiser and more genuinely religious of the two, is certainly also, as the authoress constantly makes you feel, the least happy. She is always touching gently and compassionately Mr. Farebrother's slight moral weaknesses,—his preference for comfortable drawing-rooms and whist, especially whist at which he can make certain small but steady winnings, over the duties of his calling,—his eagerness for the salary of the hospital chaplaincy, for the salary rather than for the work which should earn the salary;—and she takes pains to give the impression of spiritual *wistfulness*, rather than faith as the hidden centre of the vicar's Christianity. But the most remarkable thread of spiritual melancholy in the book constitutes the real end for which it is written,— the picture of Dorothea's beautiful and noble, but utterly unsatisfied and unresting character, and the illustration of the wreck of happiness which results from her unguided spiritual cravings. In one of the most beautiful, but also one of the most melancholy passages of this new part, Dorothea Casaubon confesses her faith, and how little she can lean on any divine power external to herself for its fulfilment. The private belief, she says, to which she clings as her only comfort, is 'that by desiring what is perfectly good, even when we don't quite know what it is and cannot do what we would, we are part of the divine power against evil,—widening the skirts of light, and making the struggle with darkness narrower.' And she goes on, 'Please not to call it [this faith] by any name. You will say it is Persian, or something else geographical. It is my life. I have found it out, and cannot part with it. I have always been finding out my religion since I was a little girl. I used to pray so much; now I hardly ever pray. I try not to have desires merely for myself, because they may not be good for others, and I have too much already.' That is exquisitely truthful and exquisitely melancholy,—the passion of a soul compelled almost to give up prayer as too exhausting, because it seems the radiation of force into a vacuum, and yet retaining all the passionate love for higher guidance in which prayer finds its source and its justification. And just as Dorothea finds no real access of spiritual strength in the religious life, beyond that which expresses itself in her desire for a religious life, so her unhappy, narrow-hearted husband finds

6

no remedy for his own smallness of life, for his jealousy, in the religious ideas which he accepts. He reflects that his recent seizure —a heart-seizure—might not mean an early death, that he might still have twenty years of work left in him to prove to the critics— Messrs. Carp and Company—who had ridiculed his mighty preparations for small achievements, that they had been mistaken. 'To convince Carp of his mistake,' says our author, 'so that he would have to eat his own words with a good deal of indigestion, would be an agreeable accident of triumphant authorship, which the prospect of living to future ages on earth, and to all eternity in Heaven, could not exclude from contemplation. Since thus the prevision of his own ever-enduring bliss could not nullify the bitter savours of irritated jealousy and vindictiveness, it is the less surprising that the probability of transient earthly bliss for other persons, when he himself should have entered into glory, had not a potently sweetening effect. If the truth should be that some undermining disease was at work within him, there might be large opportunity for some people to be the happier when he was gone; and if one of those people should be Will Ladislaw, Mr. Casaubon objected so strongly, that it seemed as if the annoyance would make part of his disembodied existence.' There you get again, not only the melancholy, but the harsh, caustic tone,—the tone which the author takes when she is disparaging a faith which she thinks vulgar as well as untrue,—the jeering tone in which she says, in describing the creatures of prey who attended old Featherstone's funeral, 'When the animals entered the Ark in pairs, one may imagine that allied species made much private remark on each other, and were tempted to think that so many forms feeding on the same store of fodder were eminently superfluous, as tending to diminish the rations. (I fear that the part played by the vultures on that occasion would be too painful for Art to represent, those birds being disadvantageously naked about the gullet, and apparently without rites and ceremonies.)' Sentences such as these give an occasional impression that George Eliot really likes jeering at human evil, which it is most painful to imagine in one who has so noble and so high a conception of good. One almost gathers that she regards the large speculative power she possesses as itself a source of pure unhappiness. The happiest creatures she draws are those who are most able, like Caleb Garth or Adam Bede, to absorb their whole minds and sink their whole energies in limited but positive duties of visible utility. Go a little higher in the scale

to a being like Dorothea, full of nobility of the highest kind, but
without a definite practical sphere, and compelled to lavish her
life on spiritual efforts to subdue her own enthusiasm, her throbbing, inward yearning for a higher life, and we are in a world of
unhappiness where rest is never found. But the height of this
unhappiness comes out in the authoress's own comments on the
universe and its structure, including in that structure its religions.
She takes side gallantly and nobly with the power that wars
against evil. The hope that she can do something on that side is
part of her life. She has found it out, and cannot part with it. But
she has a very poor hope of the issue. She sees evil, and sees it not
seldom even unmixed with good in the hearts around her, and
scoffs at the attempt to suppose that they are better than they seem.
She sees narrowness so oppressive to her that she is constantly
laughing a scornful laugh over it, and despairing of any better
euthanasia for it than its extinction. And all this makes her bitter.
She clings to the nobler course, but she cannot repress discordant
cries at the disorder of the universe and the weakness of the painfully struggling principle of good. She is a melancholy teacher—
melancholy because sceptical; and her melancholy scepticism is too
apt to degenerate into scorn.   [?R. H. HUTTON]

The Daily Telegraph, 18 June 1872

When, month by month, with wonderful punctuality, Charles
Dickens 'put forth his green leaves,' as he used to phrase it, his
current story was really a topic of the day; it seemed something
almost akin to politics and news—as if it belonged not so much to
literature but to events. Of 'Middlemarch,' now coming out less
regularly from George Eliot's great pen, the same may be said.
'Have you read the last Book?' is an almost inevitable question
in the haunts of men. But of late a certain sense of public disappointment has found utterance. There are complaints that the
instalments appear at uncertain times; that the story itself is not
intensely interesting; and that a certain vein of melancholy runs
throughout. To understand these complaints one must observe
how other writers of the day treat their readers. They supply so
many pages every month. Then they manage, as a rule, to leave
their heroine in a position of perplexity or peril. Either she has
run away from home, and is left on London Bridge with only
fourpence-halfpenny and an opera cloak; or her soul has been

softened by the charm of a dragoon, who has killed his first wife;
or she 'breaks off' clasped in the passionate embrace of her
brother-in-law, her grandfather, or other prohibited being. Here
George Eliot entirely fails; she does not consider the necessities of
the present day. We want something lively and exciting; something to take up on the road or rail, after a late breakfast, or before
a Richmond dinner; something spiced, that will tickle the mental
palate and not demand any thought. Her heroines should be rather
fast; it is not necessary that they should be immoral. But they
should be above all things unconventional, and glide from uncon-
ventionality into equivocal positions, where 'hot kisses pressed
upon burning lips'—a phrase that is sure to make the success of
any novel, however bad—suggest possibilities generally reserved
for the Divorce Court. Then the young lady, saved by some accident
from being carried off by a man, should, to save trouble, be
carried off by consumption, and die after a short career, in which
wild talk and warm desires are baulked because Mrs. Grundy forbids
English novelists, even of the fair sex, to paint too plainly what
they hint with such full suggestion. Instead of such heroines, we
have in 'Middlemarch' Englishwomen 'nobly planned.' We have
painted for us, not slangy talk, not jaunty gait, or impudent
badinage; but the very thoughts and souls of the women themselves
—women, too, worthy to be studied and observed. We do not deny
the photographic fidelity of some of the novels of fast-girl life—
they paint, no doubt, truly enough what the writers have felt,
seen, or heard; and as stories to lighten work or fill up idle hours,
they have their merits and their place. But there is something
almost profane in speaking of such stories and the works of
George Eliot in the same sentence or breath—both are called novels,
but they are not even akin. . . .

Letter from John Blackwood, 8 September 1872

Strathtyrum / St. Andrews / N.B.
September 8/72

My Dear Mrs. Lewes

The first hundred pages of Sunset and Sunrise came here last
night and instead of going to Church with the rest of the family I
sat down and have just finished reading the proof. Dorothea is
better than any sermon that ever was preached by man. It is
noble. The picture of that bleeding solitary gallant heart alone

that night in her dreary chamber is grandly moving. How one longs to help her and how beautifully you let the daylight in.

How skilfully you are unravelling that most tangled skein of trouble. I think I see my way but I am dying to see the sun fairly risen. If the rest of the M.S. was in Edinburgh I would telegraph to the printers never to stop work until it was ready to send to me. I do not wonder at such work upsetting the ordinary routine of life and consequently health. The mere reading of it has made me think with contempt of lunch, the gong for which is about to sound.

Lewes said something about changing the division of the Books. There might be a break at page 194, which would make Book 8 begin with 'In Middlemarch a wife could not long remain ignorant that the town held a bad opinion of her husband.' How exquisitely those touches relieve the graver parts. The little talk with Tantrip in 'the old tone' follows daylight delightfully in Dorothea's room.

I do hope this will find you better and the work finished. When I wrote to you yesterday with all the admiration I expressed and felt I was puzzled as to how you could 'put your house in order' but now accept from me the first instalment of the hearty congratulations and thanks the world will soon offer to you.

always yours truly
John Blackwood

The Standard, 4 December 1872

The end has now come to this singular story, which is far more than its second title implies, 'A Study of Provincial Life;' for it is a deeply-cut etching of human nature. Looking back over the long plot, we see at the beginning of the perspective a young girl standing alone, like Hermione on her pedestal, sought and beloved by a crowd. Then the valetudinarian of fifty persuades her, through her thought of duty, to become his wife. He is a bookworm, a grubber among antiquities, a ponderous pedagogue, and perpetually burdens her young life with hard quotations from the classics. This leads to the melancholy interlude during which the wife, in spite of herself and her solemn sense of right, actually waits in hope for her husband's death, and the death takes place. All the while, however, there are episodes, somewhat freely palliated by the author, of friendship rather more than friendly between the Dorothea of the romance and certain admirers. The consummation of Mr. Casaubon's history comes; he leaves all his tomes, coins, medals, and hieroglyphs behind him; but he leaves also a testament, a practical bequest of jealousy *outre tombe*, by which he binds his widow not to remarry on pain of losing the fortune she derives from him. Now commences the struggle, not so much between her love of riches and the temptations of the new, though not quite new, affections offered her, as between her attraction towards the sympathies which she has never hitherto known, together with the enjoyment of her still early bloom, and the sense she possesses that her fortune may be applied for the benefit of her fellow-creatures. The dead hand is laid upon her, and she must choose one of these two courses. Powerful inducements arise, and the conflict is wonderfully well depicted. For although many characters of the drama are uninteresting, Lydgate, Rosamond, Ladislaw, Bulstrode, Chettam, and Cadwallader, for example, these are all redeemed by the beauty of nature belonging to this woman, who refines the whole romance and leads us on to its close as by magic. So far, we think, George Eliot herself would admit that we have fairly epitomised her novel. The last volume, then, finds this adorable Dorothea in a half-happy and half-unhappy state of confusion, her conscience and her heart being at war. That unpleasant man Lydgate lies under a fearful suspicion in Middlemarch. Upon this point turns a great part of whatever there is mysterious, and there is not much, in the story. He is charged with having accepted money in order to oblige that other unpleasant person, Bulstrode, for accelerating the death of a patient by excessive administrations of opium and brandy. Moreover, he suffers under a second misfortune; he has married Rosamond, and hates her. How George Eliot could represent such a man as a hero is more than we can comprehend. Both of these scandals are abroad, and the account of the whisperings, libels, fetchings and carryings of falsehoods between shop and shop, tavern and tavern, pavement and pavement, tea party and tea party, in moral Middlemarch is admirable. Nevertheless, it resembles Dutch painting more than anything else, and is made more wearisome by a long tale of debt and embarrassment. The reader inevitably feels that he is wandering, like a traveller over a plain, in search of some relief, of some change, of something to break the ever retreating horizon of monotony. It is really impossible to enter into the narrative of dishonoured bills with anything like that feeling which our best novelists have accustomed us to entertain. . . .

The Examiner, 7 December 1872

... It is not easy to like young Ladislaw; one is tempted to think that, in marrying him, Dorothea makes nearly as great a blunder as she did in marrying Mr Casaubon. How much pleasanter it would have been for Lydgate to be her husband? But, unfortunately, things do not always go pleasantly in real life, and the fate that befalls Dorothea is very natural, though not very welcome....

The Saturday Review, 7 December 1872

... The quarrel with humanity in *Middlemarch* is its selfishness, and the quarrel with society is its hollow respectability. Human nature and society are hard things to defend; but care for self up to a point is not identical with selfishness; and respectability which pays its way and conducts itself with external propriety is not hollow in any peculiar sense. And we must say that if our young ladies, repelled by the faint and 'neutral' virtues of Celia on the one hand, and the powerfully drawn worldly Rosamond on the other, take to be Dorotheas, with a vow to dress differently from other women, and to regulate their own conduct on the system of a general disapproval of the state of things into which they are born, the world will be a less comfortable world without being a better one....

As a foil to these high sentiments, we have her sister Celia, of whom Dorothea says that she never did anything naughty since she was born, and who really never goes contrary to our sense of what is amiable and dutiful in woman; though, not being in the good graces of the author, we are not allowed to find her attractive. Less clever than Dorothea, she has more worldly wisdom, which means perhaps more instinctive perceptions; and not feeling it her duty to subvert the world, she can take her place in it naturally. But surely it is not every girl's duty to refuse the advantages and pleasures of the condition in which she finds herself because all do not share them. She is not selfish because she is serenely happy in a happy home; and if she does her best to help and alleviate the suffering within her reach, she may comfort herself in the belief that the eye of Providence never sleeps.

It is certain that nothing in human nature in the way of a virtue or a grace will stand a strict analysis unshaken. The analytical mind is logically driven into disparagement. Thus Pascal, refining upon the pervading vanity of man, holds it impossible to escape from it. 'Those who write against glory wish for the glory of having written well; those who read it wish for the glory of having read it; and I who write this have perhaps the same longing, and those who read me will have it also.' There is no escape but in the ideal. Perhaps such a state of mind almost leads to hardness where the sympathies are not active—which they are not with our author on first opening her story. Early during its progress we have at times said to ourselves, The subjects and sentiments are tragic, but not the persons; the writer does not identify herself with them. But such a writer too keenly enters into her creations not to become attached to them, and therefore sympathetic; and tenderness for human frailty, and belief in human feeling, with whatever alloy of self, give a pathos to the close which the beginning did not promise.

We have all our especial antipathies among the vices; and the hypocrisy of seeming, the 'dwelling in decencies for ever,' the cant of selfishness, are the antipathies of George Eliot. As one book of this series followed another, each seemed to say, This is your benevolence, this your learning, this your family life, this your religion! The sleek trust in Providence which easy or grasping selfishness makes its boast is the particular subject of warning and contempt. The carefully elaborated character of Bulstrode, no hypocrite of the common type, but one who sincerely hopes to flatter Divine Justice into condoning the wrong done, and permitting ill-gotten gains to prosper on condition of a certain amount of service done, is a leading instance; but most of the selfishness of *Middlemarch* shelters itself under an assumed appeal from conscience to religion. Whether it be poor Celia justifying her girl's love of pretty things under the test that the necklace she longs for won't interfere with her prayers; or Mr. Brooke excusing a political move with one of his favourite summaries—'Religion, properly speaking, is the dread of a Hereafter'; or Mrs. Waule arguing that for her brother Peter to turn his property into Blue-Coat land was flying in the face of the Almighty that had prospered him, the appeal is uniformly a cover to the real thought or motive, and, as such, a fit subject for the satirist's pen. But every man's religion may be vulgarized if the alloy is too curiously sought for. We like things in groups; our preferences and convictions are tied together by association; but it is not always fair to couple the highest of these with the lowest, as though the same amount and quality of

thought and conviction went to each. When we are told that Mrs.
Bulstrode and Mrs. Pymdale had the same preferences in silks,
patterns of underclothing, china ware, and clergymen, it does not
prove the religion represented by the clergyman to be superficial
and trivial, though it sounds so in such a conjunction. If *Middlemarch* is melancholy, it is due perhaps to its religion being all duty,
without a sufficient admixture of hope. We miss the outlook of
blue sky which is as essential to the cheerful portraiture of
humanity by the moralist as a glimpse into the open is to the
portraiture of art.

In so far as *Middlemarch* is an allegory Mr. Casaubon represents
learning as opposed to science. . . . As for Dorothea's sudden choice
of him for a husband, it is not without precedent in real life,
reminding us at once of Madame de Staël when a prodigy of
fifteen gravely proposing to her parents that she should marry
Gibbon; as fat a specimen of distinguished middle life as Mr.
Casaubon was a lean one. The more a woman has aims of her own,
and a sense of power to carry them out, the less is she guided by
the common motives and aspirations of her sex. Personally we can
acquiesce in her first choice more readily than in her second. There
are two views of Ladislaw, who, we scarcely know on what reasonable grounds, is a great favourite with the author. He charms
Dorothea by qualities exactly the reverse of her husband's; by his
passionate prodigality of statement; by his ready understanding
of her thoughts, which Mr. Casaubon always snubbed as long-
exploded opinions, if not heresies; by the sunny brightness of his
expression and hair, that seemed to shake out light when he
moved his head quickly, 'showing poor Mr. Casaubon by contrast
altogether rayless'; by his looking an incarnation of the spring
which we must suppose he typifies; by his versatility and quick
transitions of mood and feeling, being made of such impressionable
stuff that the bow of a violin drawn near him cleverly would
at one stroke change the aspect of the world for him; by his
easy unconventional manners and attitudes, and indifference to
the solid goods of life. All these are doubtless attractions. Nature
has done much for him, but duty—by which all the other characters
of the story are tested—altogether fails in him. He does what he
likes, whether right or wrong, to the end of the story; he makes no
sacrifices; even his devotion to Dorothea does not preserve him
from an unworthy flirtation with his friend Lydgate's wife. He is
happy by luck, not desert. Just as devotees of the Virgin are said

to be saved at the last moment by a medal worn or a rosary said in her honour, so the chance of his choosing the right woman to worship (though not at the right time) saves him from the consequences of idleness and mere self-pleasing; while poor Lydgate—ten times the better man—suffers not only in happiness, but in his noblest ambitions, and sinks to the lower level of a good practice and a good income because he marries and is faithful to the vain selfish creature whom Ladislaw merely flirts with. We daresay, however, it is inevitable that a grand woman who never in her life called things by the same name as other people should not match in her own degree. There is quite enough of the vagabond in Ladislaw, in spite of his remote kinship with Mr. Casaubon, to make Mrs. Cadwallader's judgment stick by one, that Dorothea might as well marry an Italian with white mice; for the author spares us nothing, and allows his enemies to sum up his genealogy —'the son of a Polish fiddler, and grandson of a thieving Jew pawnbroker.' It is the man, not his antecedents, that the ideal woman cares for. But, after all, what is the example she sets? How does it differ from the ball-room choice of any ordinary girl who takes the pleasant fellow who pleases her fancy? not that it is reasonable to require or to expect her to make the same sort of mistake twice over. This Mrs. Cadwallader—a bright bit of worldly common sense always welcome in the county circle we get pleasantly familiar with—is, however, equally caustic upon both objects of Dorothea's choice. Celia tells her that her sister marries Mr. Casaubon because he has a great soul. 'With all my heart,' she replies. 'Oh, Mrs. Cadwallader,' cries Celia, 'I don't think it can be nice to marry a man with a great soul.' 'Well, my dear, take warning. You know the look of one now; when the next comes and wants to marry you, don't accept him.'...

The Saturday Review, 21 December 1872

... Whether it be due to early bias or to a preference of taste, this Radical writer uniformly shows tenderness for a country aristocracy. She represents its members, indeed, as proud of their rank, and often insolently supercilious towards trade, and talks of the stifling oppression of the gentlewoman's life; but her satire is all playful. She likes Mrs. Cadwallader, while exposing her foibles and prejudices. Her antipathies are all bestowed on town ambitions. The people who are at the top of the tree have got something, it

seems, by the elevation, however they came there. But, admirer as
she is of energy, the energy of rising and getting on finds no
indulgence at her hand. The struggles between wholesale and
retail trade and different professional grades, the rivalries of dress
and appointments, are with her selfishness vulgar and unmitigated.
Country town society we are to suppose the worst moral school.
The accomplished Rosamond, who would so gladly have lifted
herself out of it, would, though retaining the same nature, have
been something better in the author's eyes if she had been born
among ancestral oaks and could boast a pedigree. We gather that
the nursery of the ideal woman consists in dignified and distinguished surroundings, which she renounces because all cannot
share them—a condition not adapted to the continuance of the
race. . . .

Blackwood's Magazine, December 1872

. . . It is very noteworthy how many of the best novels of the
present day touch with more or less distinctiveness upon questions
of religious belief. We set aside, of course, those many stories—
some excellent of their kind, others the veriest rubbish—which are
confessedly stories with a purpose, written to advocate some
favourite view, in which the illustration of certain theological
tenets is of the very essence of the book. In these, if we only know
the name of the writer—sometimes a fairly accurate guess may be
arrived at by merely glancing at that of the publisher—the reader
is enabled at once to forecast the kind of fare which is provided for
him, and will proceed to read or not to read according as his bias
may incline him. But even in those which assume no such didactic
office, and whose writers would fairly repudiate any such design as
proselytism, the great problems of religion, instead of being tacitly
ignored or disguised in vague generalities, are assumed as having a
momentous influence upon human life. They are not brought
prominently into the foreground, perhaps, but they are evidently
present to the mind of the writer as elements of grave importance.
If our generation be indeed so irreverent and irreligious as it is
said to be, the traces of this character are not to be found in our
highest works of fiction. If there is scepticism in them, it is
scepticism in the better sense of the word. The doubts are those of
the honest doubter; the questioning is not of a sneering or captious
kind, but has the earnest tone of the inquirer who seeks an answer.
Even if prevalent forms of belief are sometimes held up somewhat

rudely to the light, and shown to be here and there but thread-bare spiritual raiment, it is without prejudice to the living body of truth which they are intended to clothe.

This is peculiarly the case with the works of the writer whose last production lies before us. Theological colour these volumes have none. Professions of a creed may seem to be even purposely avoided. But no one can say that their tones is other than reverent on religious questions. The unrealities of religion, whether they take the shape of formal act or fluent profession, are touched with a satire whose lash is not the less cutting because it is laid on with the most delicate wrist-play. People 'whose celestial intimacies seem not to improve their domestic manners,' who contrive 'to conciliate piety and worldliness, the nothingness of this life and the desirability of cut glass, the consciousness at once of filthy rags and the best damask,' find no mercy here. And whether the old miser Peter Featherstone seeks, as he declares in his will, 'to please God Almighty' by building almshouses, or Mr. Bulstrode attempts 'an act of restitution which may move Divine Providence to avert painful consequences,' the touch of honest scorn in the brief phrases is more effective than a homily. And nowhere, read where we will, shall we find less religious narrowness, or a fuller confession of the spiritual needs of human nature. Indeed, the cry of the soul after something more satisfying than the mere husks of worldly well-doing and success seems uttered in these volumes with an intensity which is almost painful. True, we have no distinct ideal set up and recommended as really attainable; rather—and this gives to the work that remarkable tinge of melancholy which has been remarked, in spite of all their grace and humour, in most of its predecessors from the same hand—we are allowed to gather that for the most part ideals are unattainable, and that the highest aspirations only serve to give a grandeur to the failure in which they inevitably end. We have been forcibly reminded, as we read, of the tone of thought which runs through several of those most remarkable sermons of Frederick Robertson—that all life is in one sense an illusion and a failure: and that the Highest Life on earth was, to outward seeming, a notorious failure. Take the characters in these volumes: all who set before them an object in life higher than their fellows, fail in its attainment. Casaubon is a failure, Dorothea is a failure, Lydgate is a failure more than all. It might seem, at first thought, as though the moral were as cynical as this —if you would escape disappointment, you must not seek to rise above the level of your fellow-creatures. It is Celia, with her kitten-like content and hatred of 'notions,'—Sir James Chettam, who 'doesn't go much into ideas,'—Will Ladislaw, with his amiable vagabond dilettantism, who looks upon all forms of prescribed work as 'harness,' and holds genius to be 'necessarily intolerant of fetters,'—Fred Vincy, with his goodhumoured gentlemanlike selfishness,—who come out, on the whole, with the largest share of commonplace happiness. But we are much mistaken if such be the moral which the author—if any moral be intended or permissible—would have us draw. The lines may be read another way. To have an ideal at which we aim, and that ideal of the highest kind, is the worthy life and the true life, though not of necessity that which attains its object or wins content. It is better to fail than to succeed, if the aim has been noble in the one case, and mean in the other. . . .

REV. W. LUCAS COLLINS

The Academy, 1 January 1873

. . . As 'a study of provincial life,' if it were nothing more, *Middle-march* would have a lasting charm for students of human nature in its less ephemeral costumes; besides the crowds of men and women whom we have all known in real life, where, however, to our dimmer vision, they seemed less real and life-like than in the book, the relations between the different clusters, the proportions in which the different elements mix, the points of contact and the degree of isolation in the different ranks; the contented coexistence of town and county, the channels of communication between the two always open and yet so rarely used, the effect of class distinctions in varying the mental horizon and obliging the most matter-of-fact observer to see a few things in perspective,—all the subtle factors which make up the character of a definite state of society are given with inimitable accuracy and fulness of insight. The picture in its main outlines is as true of the England of to-day or the England of a hundred years ago as of the England of the Reform agitation. The world as we know it has its wise and good, its fools and hypocrites scattered up and down a neutral-tinted mass in much the same proportion as at Middlemarch. The only difference is that they are not so plainly recognisable, and this is perhaps the reason that a first perusal of the book seems to have an almost oppressive effect on ordinary readers, somewhat as little children are frightened at a live automaton toy. It is not natural to most men to know so much of their fellow-creatures as George Eliot shows them, to penetrate behind the scenes in so many homes, to understand the motives of ambiguous conduct, to watch 'like gods knowing good and evil' the tangled course of intermingled lives, the remote mainsprings of impulse and the wide-eddying effects of action. Even with the author's assistance it is not easy to maintain the same height of observant wisdom for long, and since the intricacy of the subject is real, a feeling of even painful bewilderment in its contemplation is not entirely unbecoming.

But the complicated conditions of so seemingly simple a thing as provincial life are not the main subject of the work. The busy idleness of Middlemarch, its trade, its politics, its vestry meetings, and its neighbouring magnates, only form the background of relief to two or three spiritual conflicts, the scenery amongst which two or three souls spend some eventful years in working out their own salvation and their neighbours', or in effecting, with equal labour, something less than salvation for both. The story of these conflicts and struggles is the thread which unites the whole, and sympathy with its incidents is the force that reconciles the reader to the unwonted strain upon his intellectual faculties already noticed; and to the yet further effort necessary to recognise the fact that the real and the ideal sides of our common nature do coexist in just such relations, and with just such proportionate force as the author reveals. For, without this admission, it is impossible to appreciate the full literary and artistic perfection of the work as a whole; some readers may delight spontaneously in the author's moral earnestness, and only admire her satirical insight, while others delight in her satire and coldly admit the excellence of the moral purpose; but the two are only opposite aspects of the same large theory of the universe, which is at once so charitable and so melancholy that it would be fairly intolerable (although true) without the sauce of an unsparing humour.

Middlemarch is the story of two rather sad fatalities, of two lives which, starting with more than ordinary promise, had to rest content with very ordinary achievement, and could not derive unmixed consolation from the knowledge, which was the chief prize of their struggles, that failure is never altogether undeserved. One of the original mottoes to the first book gives the clue to what follows:

'*1st Gent.* Our deeds are fetters that we forge ourselves.

2nd Gent. Ay, truly; but I think it is the world
That brings the iron:'

but as the action proceeds a further consciousness gathers shape: 'It always remains true that if we had been greater, circumstances would have been less strong against us;' which is still more simply expressed in Dorothea's 'feeling that there was always something better which she might have done, if she had only been better and known better.' The two failures, however, have little in common but their irrevocable necessity. From one point of view, Dorothea's is the most tragical, for the fault in her case seems to be altogether in the nature and constitution of the universe; her devotion and purity of intention are altogether beautiful, even when, for lack of knowledge, they are expended in what seems to be the wrong place, but it is a sad reflection that their beauty must always rest on a basis of illusion because there is no right place for their bestowal. Except in the chapter of her marriages Dorothea is a perfect woman, but for a perfect woman any marriage is a *mésalliance*, and as such, 'certainly those determining acts of her life were not ideally beautiful.' But we can as little tell as the Middlemarchers 'what else that was in her power she ought rather to have done.' If she had had no illusions she might have been a useful Lady Bountiful, managing her own affairs like Goethe's Theresa, a personage who inspires but mediocre interest, and might have married Mrs. Cadwallader's philanthropic Lord Triton without suspicion of *mésalliance*: but then she would not have been Dorothea, not the impetuous young woman with 'a heart large enough for the Virgin Mary,' whose sighs, when she thinks her lover is untrue, are breathed for 'all the troubles of all the people on the face of the earth.' The world must be ugly for her power of seeing it as it is not to be beautiful, just as men's lives must be sad and miserable to call for the exercise of her infinite charity. Still the illusions are sweet and the charity beneficent, and since women like Dorothea are content to live only for others, life may offer occasions enough for self-sacrifice to compensate them for the natural impossibility of shaping an ideally perfect course through the multitudinous imperfections of real existence. It would be ungenerous to accept such a fate for them without reluctance, and therefore some sadness must always mix with our thoughts of the historic and unhistoric Dorotheas of the world; but it is also true that the moral force exercised by such characters can no more be wasted than any physical impulse, and that, without the disinterested virtue of the few, the conflicting appetites of a world of Rosamonds would make life impossible. To keep society alive is

perhaps a worthier mission than to cheer the declining years of
Mr. Casaubon; but to do more than keep it alive, to make it a
fit home for future Dorotheas, the present supply of such mission-
aries would have to be increased; and they are born, not made.
Perhaps the strongest example of the author's instinctive truthfulness is that she never loses sight of the limits to the exercise of
the power which she represents so vividly and values so highly. A
life's growth of empty egotism like Mr. Casaubon's cannot be
melted in a year of marriage, even to Dorothea; with a generous
example close before her, Rosamond can be almost honest for once
at little expense, but she can no more change her character than
her complexion or the colour of her eyes, or than she can unmake
the whole series of circumstances which have made her life less
negatively innocent than Celia's. A little more selfishness, a little
more obstinacy, a little less good fortune, and especially life in a
just lower moral atmosphere, make all the difference between a
pretty, prosaic, kittenish wife and a kind of well-conducted
domestic vampire. It is by such contrasts as these that George
Eliot contrives to preach tolerance even while showing with grim
distinctness the ineffaceableness of moral distinctions and the
unrelenting force of moral obligations. If virtue is a matter of
capacity, defect only calls for pity; but defects which we do not
venture to blame may be none the less fatal to the higher life, while
the smallest shoot of virtue, if the heavens and earth chance to be
propitious to its growth, may spread into a stately tree.

Such at least is the inference suggested by another contrast,
that between Lydgate and Fred, for though marriage appears the
'determining act' in their lives also, it is itself determined by
certain essential points of character and disposition. Fred's honest
boyish affection for a girl who is a great deal too good for him
brings its own reward, as that kind of virtue often will; there was
enough self-abandonment in it to deserve a generous answer, and
in the long-run people generally get their deserts. The failure of
Lydgate's intellectual aspirations, as the consequence of a marriage
contracted altogether at the bidding of his lower nature, is of course
much more elaborately treated than Fred's simple 'love-problem.'
Unlike most of the other characters, Lydgate does not become
thoroughly intelligible till the last number of the work has been
read in connection with the first: then he appears as a masculine
counterpart to Dorothea with the relative proportions of head and
heart reversed. But while it was abstractedly impossible for

Dorothea to be altogether wise, without detriment to the peculiar and charming character of her goodness, there was nothing but concrete human infirmity to prevent Lydgate from combining the mind of Bichat and the morals of Fred Vincy. Instead of such a compound the actual and very human Lydgate is one of those men whose lives are cut in two, whose intellectual interests have no direct connection with their material selves, and who only discover the impossibility of living according to habit or tradition when brought by accident or their own heedlessness face to face with difficulties that require thought as well as resolution. There was not room in the life he contemplated for a soul much larger than Rosamond's, and it may be doubted whether the Rosamond he wished for would not, by a merely passive influence, have been as obstructive to his wide speculations, for he was just, though not expansive, and the duties entailed by one act of weakness may multiply and branch as much as if they were of a valuable stock. On the other hand, if the scientific ardour had been more absorbing he might have gone on his own way, crushing all poor Rosamond's little schemes of opposition, and then she would have been the victim instead of the oppressor, but his character would have been as far from ideal excellence as before. The interest culminates when Lydgate, entangled with the consequences of his own and other people's wrongdoing, finds in Dorothea the beneficent influence that spends itself in setting straight whatever is not constitutionally crooked, but he has also of course found out by then that the events which led him to cross her path were the same that had proved fatal to his aspirations; the enlarged sympathies were gathered during the process that paralysed his original activity. The story of a man 'who has not done what he once meant to do' has always a strong element of pathos, but when what he meant to do was not in itself impossible, like the realization of Dorothea's visions, there remains a twofold consolation; if possible in itself, and yet not done as proposed, it must have been impossible to the proposer, and therefore his failure is free from blame, while disappointment of his hopes, though painful, cannot be regarded as an unmitigated evil, since such fallen aspirations as Lydgate's are still something it is better to have had than to be altogether without. Natural fatality and the logic of facts are made to persuade us that all regrets are unpractical except the most unpractical of all—'if we had only known better and been better'—but the first step towards solving a problem is to state it; and one of the many merits of

7

Middlemarch is that it shows the inadequacy of all other less arduous short cuts to the reformation of society. Ordinary mortals who are not fatalists have no excuse for calling a book sad which makes the redress of every one's wrongs rest in the last resort with themselves: while people whose idea of the world is already as gloomy as it well can be, cannot fail to derive some consolation from the thought that George Eliot's wider knowledge and juster perceptions find here and there a little to admire as well as much everywhere to laugh at.   H. LAWRENNY

The Fortnightly Review, 19 January 1873

Fifteen months of pausing and recurring literary excitement are at an end; and 'Middlemarch,' the chief English book of the immediate present, lies complete before us. Now that we have the book as a whole, what place does it seem to take among the rest with which its illustrious writer has enriched, I will not say posterity, because for posterity every present is apt in turn to prove itself a shallow judge, but her own generation and us who delight to honour her?

In the sense in which anything is called ripe because of fullness and strength, I think the last of George Eliot's novels is also the ripest. 'Middlemarch' is extraordinarily full and strong, even among the company to which it belongs. And though I am not sure that it is the property of George Eliot's writing to satisfy, its property certainly is to rouse and attach, in proportion to its fullness and strength. There is nothing in the literature of the day so rousing—to the mind of the day there is scarcely anything so rousing in all literature—as her writing is. What she writes is so full of her time. It is observation, imagination, pathos, wit and humour, all of a high class in themselves; but what is more, all saturated with modern ideas, and poured into a language of which every word bites home with peculiar sharpness to the contemporary consciousness. That is what makes it less safe than it might seem at first sight to speak for posterity in such a case. We are afraid of exaggerating the meaning such work will have for those who come after us, for the very reason that we feel its meaning so pregnant for ourselves. If, indeed, the ideas of to-day are certain to be the ideas of to-morrow and the day after, if scientific thought and the positive synthesis are indubitably to rule the world, then any one, it should seem, might speak boldly enough to George Eliot's place.

For the general definition of her work, I should say, is precisely this—that, among writers of the imagination, she has taken the lead in expressing and discussing the lives and ways of common folks—*votum, timor, ira, voluptas*—in terms of scientific thought and the positive synthesis. She has walked between two epochs, upon the confines of two worlds, and has described the old in terms of the new. To the old world belong the elements of her experience, to the new world the elements of her reflection on experience. The elements of her experience are the 'English Provincial Life' before the Reform Bill—the desires and alarms, indignations and satisfactions, of the human breast in county towns and villages, farms and parsonages, manor-houses, counting-houses, surgeries, streets and lanes, shops and fields, of midlands unshaken in their prejudices and unvisited by the steam-engine. To the new world belong the elements of her reflection; the many-sided culture which looks back upon prejudice with analytical amusement; the philosophy which declares the human family deluded in its higher dreams, dependent upon itself, and bound thereby to a closer if a sadder brotherhood; the habit in regarding and meditating physical laws, and the facts of sense and life, which leads up to that philosophy and belongs to it; the mingled depth of bitterness and tenderness in the human temper of which the philosophy becomes the spring.

Thus there is the most pointed contrast between the matter of these English tales and the manner of their telling. The matter is antiquated in our recollections, the manner seems to anticipate the future of our thoughts. Plenty of other writers have taken hum-drum and narrow aspects of English life with which they were familiar, and by delicacy of perception and justness of rendering have put them together into pleasant works of literary art, without running the matter into a manner out of direct correspondence with it. But this procedure of George Eliot's is a newer thing in literature, and infinitely harder to judge of, than the gray and tranquil harmonies of that other mode of art. For no writer uses so many instruments in riveting the interest of the cultivated reader about the characters, and springs of character, which she is exhibiting. First, I say, she has the perpetual application of her own intelligence to the broad problems and conclusions of modern thought. That, for instance, when Fred Vincy, having brought losses upon the Garth family, feels his own dishonour more than their suffering, brings the reflection how '*we are most of us brought up in the notion that the highest motive for not doing a wrong is something irrespective of the beings who would suffer the wrong.*' That again, a few pages later, brings the humorous allusions to Caleb Garth's classification of human employments, into business, politics, preaching, learning, and amusement, as one which '*like the categories of more celebrated men, would not be acceptable in these more advanced times.*' And that makes it impossible to describe the roguery of a horse-dealer without suggesting that he '*regarded horse-dealing as the finest of the arts, and might have argued plausibly that it had nothing to do with morality.*'

Next, this writer possesses, in her own sympathetic insight into the workings of human nature, a psychological instrument which will be perpetually displaying its power, its subtlety and trenchancy, in passages like this which lays bare the working of poor Mrs. Bulstrode's faithful mind upon the revelation of her husband's guilt: 'Along with her brother's looks and words, there darted into her mind the idea of some guilt in her husband. Then, under the working of terror, came the image of her husband exposed to disgrace; *and then, after an instant of scorching shame in which she only felt the eyes of the world, with one leap of her heart she was at his side in mournful but unreproaching fellowship with shame and isolation.*' Of the same trenchancy and potency, equally subtle and equally sure of themselves, are a hundred other processes of analysis, whether applied to serious crises—like that prolonged one during which Bulstrode wavers before the passive murder which shall rid him of his one obstacle as an efficient servant of God—or to such trivial crises as occur in the experiences of a Mrs. Dollop or a Mrs. Taft, or others who, being their betters, still belong to the class of 'well-meaning women knowing very little of their own motives.' And this powerful knowledge of human nature is still only one of many instruments for exposing a character and turning it about. What the character itself thinks and feels, exposed by this, will receive a simultaneous commentary in what the modern analytic mind has to remark upon such thoughts and feelings: see a good instance in the account (at page 98 of Book III.) of Mr. Casaubon's motives before marriage and experiences after it.

Then, the writer's studies in science and physiology will constantly come in to suggest for the spiritual processes of her personages an explanation here or an illustration there. For a stroke of overwhelming power in this kind, take what is said in one place of Bulstrode—that 'he shrank from a direct lie with an intensity disproportionate to the number of his more indirect misdeeds. *But many of these misdeeds were like the subtle muscular movements which are not taken account of in the consciousness; though they bring about the end that we fix in our minds and desire. And it is only what we are vividly conscious of that we can vividly imagine to be seen by Omniscience.*'

And it is yet another instrument which the writer handles when she seizes on critical points of physical look and gesture in her personages, in a way which is scientific and her own. True, there are many descriptions, and especially of the beauty and gestures of Dorothea—and these are written with a peculiarly loving and as it were watchful exquisiteness—which may be put down as belonging to the ordinary resources of art. But look at Caleb Garth; he is a complete physiognomical study in the sense of Mr. Darwin, with the 'deepened depression in the outer angle of his bushy eyebrows, which gave his face a peculiar mildness;' with his trick of 'broadening himself by putting his thumbs into his arm-holes,' and the rest. Such are Rosamond's ways of turning her neck aside and patting her hair when she is going to be obstinate. So, we are not allowed to forget 'a certain massiveness in Lydgate's manner and tone, corresponding with his physique;' nor indeed, any point of figure and physiognomy which strike the author's imagination as symptomatic. Symptomatic is the best word. There is a medical strain in the tissue of the story. There is a profound sense of the importance of physiological conditions in human life. But further still, I think, there is something like a medical habit in the writer, of examining her own creations for their symptoms, which runs through her descriptive and narrative art and gives it some of its peculiar manner.

So that, apart from the presence of rousing thought in general maxims and allusions, we know now what we mean when we speak of the fullness and strength derived, in the dramatic and narrative part of the work, from the use of so many instruments as we have seen. Then comes the question, do these qualities satisfy us as thoroughly as they rouse and interest? Sometimes I think they do, and sometimes not. Nothing evidently can be more satisfying, more illuminating, than that sentence which explained, by a primitive fact in the experimental relations of mind and body, a peculiar kind of bluntness in the conscience of the religious Bulstrode. And generally, wherever the novelist applies her philosophy or science to serious purposes, even if it may be applied too often, its effect seems to me good. But in lighter applications I doubt if the same kind of thing is not sometimes mistaken. The wit and humour of this writer every one of us knows and has revelled in; I do not think these want to gain body from an elaborate or semi-scientific language. In the expression of fun or common observation, is not such language apt to read a little technical and heavy, like a kind of intellectual slang? I do not think the delightful fun about Mrs. Garth and Mary and the children gains by it. I doubt if it is in place when it is applied to the mental processes of Mrs. Dollop or Mr. Bambridge. And when, for example, we are asked to consider what would have happened if Fred Vincy's 'prophetic soul had been urged to particularize,' that is what I mean by something like a kind of intellectual slang.

But all this only concerns some methods or processes of the writer, picked from random points in the development of her new story and its characters. What of these in themselves? Well, there comes back the old sense, of a difference to the degree to which we are roused, attached, and taught, and the degree to which we are satisfied. The book is full of high feeling, wisdom, and acuteness. It contains some of the most moving dramatic scenes in our literature. A scene like that of Dorothea in her night of agony, a scene like that in which the greatness of her nature ennobles for a moment the smallness of Rosamond's, is consummate alike in conception and in style. The characters are admirable in their vigour and individuality, as well as in the vividness and fullness of illustration with which we have seen that they are exhibited. Dorothea with her generous ardour and ideal cravings; Mr. Brooke with his good-natured viewy incoherency and self-complacence; Celia with her narrow worldly sense seasoned by affectionateness; Chettam with his honourable prejudices; Ladislaw with his dispersed ambitions, and the dispositions and susceptibilities of his origin; Casaubon with his learning which is lumber, his formalism and inaccessibility of character, his distrust of himself and other people; Lydgate with his solid ambitions which fail, and his hollow which succeed; Rosamond 'with that hard slight thing called girlishness,' and all the faults which can underlie skin-deep graces; Bulstrode with the piety designed in vain to propitiate the chastisement of destiny; the witty unscrupulous rattle of Mrs. Cadwallader; the Garth household, the Farebrother household, the Vincys, the country bankers and country tradesmen, the rival practitioners, the horse-dealer, the drunkard who is the ghost of Bulstrode's ancient sin—all these are living and abiding additions to every one's circle of the familiar acquaintances that importune not. But as one turns them over in one's mind or talk, them and their fortunes in the book, with laughter or sympathy or pity or indignation or love, there will arise all sorts of questionings, debatings, such as do not arise after a reading which has left the mind satisfied. One calls in question this or that point in the conduct of the story; the attitude which the writer personally assumes towards her own creations; the general lesson which seems to underlie her scheme; above all, the impression which its issue leaves upon oneself.

The questions one asks are such as, within limits like these, it would be idle to attempt to solve, or even to state, except in the most fragmentary way. Are not, for instance, some points in the story a little coarsely invented and handled? At the very outset, is not the hideous nature of Dorothea's blind sacrifice too ruthlessly driven home to us, when it ought to have been allowed to reveal itself by gentler degrees? Is it not too repulsive to talk of the moles on Casaubon's face, and to make us loathe the union from the beginning? Is not the formalism and dryness of Casaubon's nature a little overdone in his first conversation and his letter of courtship? Or again, is not the whole intrigue of Ladislaw's birth and Bulstrode's guilt, the Jew pawnbroker and Raffles, somewhat common and poor? The story is made to hinge twice, at two important junctures, upon the incidents of watching by a death-bed. Is that scant invention, or is it a just device for bringing out, under nearly parallel circumstances, the opposite characters of Mary Garth and of Bulstrode—her untroubled and decisive integrity under difficulties, his wavering conscience, which, when to be passive is already to be a murderer, permits itself at last in something just beyond passiveness? Or, to shift the ground of question, does not the author seem a little unwarrantably hard upon some of her personages and kind to others? Fred and Rosamond Vincy, for instance—one would have said there was not so much to choose. The author, however, is on the whole kind to the brother, showing up his faults but not harshly, and making him in the end an example of how an amiable spendthrift may be redeemed by a good man's help and a good girl's love. While to the sister, within whose mind 'there was not room enough for luxuries to look small in,' she shows a really merciless animosity, and gibbets her as an example of how an unworthy wife may degrade the career of a

man of high purposes and capacities. Celia, too, who is not really
so very much higher a character, the author makes quite a pet of
in comparison, and puts her in situations where all her small
virtues tell; and so on. Minute differences of character for better
or worse may justly be shown, of course, as producing vast
differences of effect under the impulsion of circumstances. Still, I
do not think it is altogether fancy to find wanting here the
impartiality of the greatest creators towards their mind's offspring.

Then, for the general lesson of the book, it is not easy to feel
quite sure what it is, or how much importance the author gives it.
In her prelude and conclusion both, she seems to insist upon the
design of illustrating the necessary disappointment of a woman's
nobler aspirations in a society not made to second noble aspirations
in a woman. And that is one of the most burning lessons which any
writer could set themselves to illustrate. But then, Dorothea does
not suffer in her ideal aspirations from yielding to the pressure of
social opinion. She suffers in them from finding that what she has
done, in marrying an old scholar in the face of social opinion, was
done under a delusion as to the old scholar's character. 'Exactly,'
is apparently the author's drift; 'but it is society which so nurtures
women that their ideals cannot but be ideals of delusion.' Taking
this as the author's main point (and I think prelude and conclusion
leave it still ambiguous), there are certainly passages enough in the
body of the narrative which point the same remonstrance against
what society does for women. '*The shallowness of a water-nixie's
soul may have a charm till she becomes didactic:*' that describes the
worthlessness of what men vulgarly prize in women. '*In the British
climate there is no incompatibility between scientific insight and
furnished lodgings. The incompatibility is chiefly between scientific
ambition and a wife who objects to that kind of residence.*' That points
to the rarity of a woman, as women are brought up, who prefers
the things of the mind to luxury. '"*Of course she is devoted to her
husband,*" said Rosamond, implying a notion of necessary sequence
which the scientific man regarded as the prettiest possible for a woman.'
That points with poignant irony to the science, as to the realities
of society and the heart, of men whose science is solid in other
things.

It is perhaps in pursuance of the same idea that Dorothea's
destiny, after Casaubon has died, and she is free from the consequences of a first illusory ideal, is not made very brilliant after

all. She cannot be an Antigone or a Theresa. She marries the man of her choice, and bears him children; but we have been made to feel all along that he is hardly worthy of her. There is no sense of triumph in it; there is rather a sense of sadness in a subdued and restricted, if not now a thwarted destiny. In this issue there is a deep depression; there is that blending of the author's bitterness with her profound tenderness of which I have already spoken. And upon this depends, or with it hangs together, that feeling of uncertainty and unsatisfiedness as to the whole fable and its impression which remains with the reader when all is done. He could spare the joybells—the vulgar upshot of happiness for ever after—Sophia surrendered to the arms of her enraptured Jones— if he felt quite sure of the moral or intellectual point of view which had dictated so chastened and subdued a conclusion. As it is, he does not feel clear enough about the point of view, the lesson, the main moral and intellectual outcome, to put up with that which he feels to be uncomfortable in the combinations of the story, and flat in the fates of friends and acquaintances who have been brought so marvellously near to him.

That these and such like questionings should remain in the mind, after the reading of a great work of fiction, would in ordinary phrase be said to indicate that, however great the other qualities of the work, it was deficient in qualities of art. The fact is, that this writer brings into her fiction so many new elements, and gives it pregnancy and significance in so many unaccustomed directions, that it is presumptuousness to pronounce in that way as to the question of art. Certainly, it is possible to write with as little illusion, or with forms of disillusion much more cynical, as to society and its dealings and issues, and yet to leave a more har- monious and definite artistic impression than is here left. French writers perpetually do so. But then George Eliot, with her science and her disillusion, has the sense of bad and good as the great French literary artists have not got it, and is taken up, as they are not, with the properly moral elements of human life and struggling. They exceed in all that pertains to the passions of the individual; she cares more than they do for the general beyond the individual. That it is by which she rouses—I say rouses, attaches, and elevates —so much more than they do, even if her combinations satisfy much less. Is it, then, that a harmonious and satisfying literary art is impossible under these conditions? Is it that a literature, which confronts all the problems of life and the world, and recognises all the springs of action, and all that clogs the springs, and all that comes from their smooth or impeded working, and all the importance of one life for the mass,—is it that such a literature must be like life itself, to leave us sad and hungry?

[SIDNEY COLVIN]

The Edinburgh Review, January 1873

... This realistic treatment of human aspirations and illusions must recall to every one familiar with European literature the images of disappointment and despair with which Balzac has peopled the imagination of our times. But, as in the person of 'Felix Holt,' and the 'Compagnon du Tour de France,' we are far more conscious of the discrepancies than of the resemblances between the artisan of George Eliot and the 'ouvrier' of George Sand, so here we feel that the satirical ἦθος of the writers is very distinct. They are both sad chroniclers of the weakness of our race —both, either from love of truth or pride in a higher intuition, have a pleasure in raising aloft the hopes and feelings of mankind, and then leaving them to themselves, to find their end just as they would in the pitiless and inconstant world, with little for the novelist to preach about, but with much for the tears of women and gentler thoughts of men. But while in Balzac there is ever the diabolic consciousness of the corruptions of the world, at once casting a glamour over evil in the mind of others and vindicating it in our own, George Eliot and George Sand are inspired with a generous pity for their own creations, and whilst they punish are content to do their best to pardon.

The Times, 7 March 1873

For a year and more the reading world was kept in suspense while *Middlemarch* appeared in monthly or bi-monthly numbers. According to custom on such high occasions, it was served out a few chapters at a time, and readers were expected to accept with thankfulness the portion vouchsafed to them, to read it, and to go about their business with the equanimity of the Sultan in the *Arabian Nights*, who, instead of threatening to cut off Scheherazade's head if she did not immediately finish her story, was content to wait till the time came round when the watchful sister, whom we may interpret to mean the publisher, suggested that it should be continued. We confess that our patience was not quite so

Oriental; but, now that we have the whole book in our hands, we forgive Messrs. Blackwood for tantalizing us, and we feel that the splendid novel which was able to keep us interested for so many months is at least as great a treat in the second reading as in the first. Knowing the story as a whole, we can now begin to study it in every part. There is a new delight in the close observation of its admirable art, in the full understanding of its weighty sentences. It is a luxury to pause upon each passage of fine, well-woven English, never a mere web of words. We do not now look towards the end, wondering whether this or that will happen, but we search the pages for riches we have missed. There are few novels in the language which will repay reading over again so well as *Middlemarch*. . . .

In reading *Middlemarch*, as in George Eliot's other stories, nothing strikes us more than the topographical power, if we may so call it, of her writing. She bestows upon the places the same attention she bestows upon persons, and the pictures of a county town and a country side created in the imagination of the reader are no less clear and distinct than the pictures of the men and women with whom they are peopled. This 'bump of locality' in her genius encircles the persons of the story with a background and scenery the colour and perspective of which double the reality of the drama. By frequent touches, rather than by detailed descriptions, the arrangement and distances of streets and roads, the look of fields and buildings, the relative positions of villages and hamlets, are conveyed to us, so that before we have got far in the novel we are able to find our way from Middlemarch to Lowick, and from Lowick to Freshitt, and have not the bewildering feeling of being taken blindfolded from place to place. The face of the country becomes familiar to us, till we know what sort of things they are which 'make the gamut of joy in landscape to midland-bred souls—the things they toddled among, or perhaps learned by heart standing between their father's knees, while he drove leisurely.'. . . Dorothea is the chief heroine, and so far the lesson of her fate is the moral of the tale; but its variety and interest are not subordinated to a single meaning, though a meaning may be expressed at the beginning and the end. The 'Prelude' strikes a key-note by reminding us of that early episode in the life of St. Theresa, when the little girl, hand-in-hand with her still smaller brother, toddled out from rugged Avila to seek martyrdom in the country of the Moors. They were turned back from their great resolve 'by domestic reality in the shape of uncles,' but their child-pilgrimage was a fit beginning.

'Theresa's passionate, ideal nature demanded an epic life. What were many-volumed romances of chivalry, and the social conquests of a brilliant girl to her? Her flame quickly burned up that light fuel, and, fed from within, soared after some illimitable satisfaction.'

Dorothea is 'a later-born St. Theresa,' but the epic life she attempts turns out, at least for a considerable part of it, 'a tragic failure.' Her vague longings lead her to make very definite mistakes, the chief of which is the marrying of an elderly pedant out of enthusiasm for his musty learning and superannuated researches. She is nevertheless a noble woman, and her blundering life is held up to us as due to 'the inconvenient indefiniteness with which the Supreme Power has fashioned the natures of women,' permitting exceptions to the general type, for whom the common social lot is not enough.

'Here and there a cygnet is reared uneasily among the ducklings in the brown pond, and never finds the living stream in fellowship with its own oary-footed kind. Here and there is born a St. Theresa, foundress of nothing, whose loving heartbeats and sobs after an unattained goodness tremble off and are dispersed among hindrances, instead of centring in some long-recognizable deed.'

There is a certain school which will find satisfaction in thinking that Dorothea's story involves some special impeachment of the fitness of the present female lot. We do not think that this is at all intended, and if it be intended it is certainly not justified. George Eliot gives us a noble portrait and an affecting history of a woman who nearly spoilt her life by attempting to rise above her opportunities, but her failures and mistakes are not due to the fact of her being a woman, but are simply those which belong to the common lot of human life. Just as she married a husband who did not suit her, so a man may marry a wife who does not suit him. The mistakes which arose out of her vague longings, her desire 'to shape her thought and deed in noble agreement,' were not one whit sillier or more lamentable than those which a young man may fall into under the like circumstances. The fetters she wore are too common to humanity, but the weight of them is felt far more by

men than by women. Youths more often than girls long after a
life of 'far resonant action' and find it not; unsatisfied ambitions
are masculine rather than female ills; and, as a matter of fact,
women attain contentment and their ideal far oftener than men.
Yet, while we demur to any special application of the story of this
new St. Theresa, we allow that its pathos and force would be half
lost if she were not a woman. In her portrait, womanhood, beauty,
and the ardour of a tender, yet masculine, spirit are wrought
together with thorough art, and her mistakes, her endurance, her
failures, and her triumphs must touch and thrill and fascinate us
with a double power, because they are those of a woman. The
reader is strangely attracted to this young creature, who knew
Pascal and Jeremy Taylor by heart, to whom 'the destinies of
mankind, seen by the light of Christianity, made the solicitudes of
female fashion appear an occupation for Bedlam;' whose soul and
eyes were so full of candour, who was possessed by such a frank
ardour, such a generous anxiety to do what was right, such a
passion for truth and justice in all things, even when the terrible
oppression of the adverse circumstances of her life was crushing
her spirit. She is drawn with a unity of conception all the more
perfect because of the faults with which her physical and mental
beauty are slightly and subtly touched. That she should be somewhat shortsighted, and that she should be cold to the influences
of art, wandering careless through the galleries of the Vatican,
though Rome was not without its 'gigantic broken revelations,'
are traits which seem perfectly in keeping directly they are
mentioned. She begins by worshipping her scholastic husband, and
we are finely shown how, under the cold contact of his formal
nature, her feelings changed 'with the secret motion of a watch-
hand from what they had been in her maiden dream.' Many of the
finest passages in the novel relate to her. Of these is the account
of her interview with Lydgate about her husband's heart disease,
wonderful for its concentrated pathos, and for its quick and subtle
pursuit of thought and feeling through Dorothea's mind. Not less
masterly is the analysis of her feelings and the description of her
conduct towards the withered scholar, which ends the second
volume; or, in the fourth volume, and after Casaubon's death, the
description of her behaviour upon finding Rosamond and
Ladislaw together, of 'the great draught of scorn' which sustained
her through the day, and of the reaction which followed when she
was shut up alone in her room:—

'Then came the hour in which the waves of suffering shook her too thoroughly to leave any power of thought. She could only cry in loud whispers, between her sobs, after her lost belief which she had planted and kept alive from a very little seed since the days in Rome—after her lost joy of clinging with silent love and faith to one who, misprized by others, was worthy in her thought; after her lost woman's pride of reigning in his memory; after her sweet dim perspective of hope, that along some pathway they should meet with unchanged recognition, and take up the backward years as a yesterday.

'In that hour she repeated what the merciful eyes of solitude have looked on for ages in the spiritual struggles of man: she besought hardness and coldness and aching weariness to bring her relief from the mysterious incorporeal might of her anguish; she lay on the bare floor and let the night grow cold around her, while her grand woman's frame was shaken by sobs as if she had been a despairing child.'

Perhaps the finest passage in the whole novel is the description of her second interview with Rosamond, a few pages further on. Our limits will not suffer us to extract it, but it must be familiar to most of our readers, and they will agree with us that George Eliot's works do not contain a more admirable instance of the intuitive power which seems to guide her genius along the windings of the human mind. It would be hard, also, to match the dramatic effectiveness of the situation, the natural course of the dialogue, the fine tact, the tenderness and felicity of touch and expression, the simplicity and power of the whole writing of the chapter which at last brings Dorothea and Ladislaw together at the end of the book.

He was her second husband, and she married him for love, as she had married Casaubon for learning. His character is drawn with much care and subtlety, yet there is a certain indistinctness about his picture; neither does he seem at all worthy of the woman he wins. This may only be because the reader is in love with her himself, or because George Eliot altogether declines to allow a magnificent destiny even to Dorothea. She loses most of her fortune by her second marriage, and though in time Ladislaw is successful and gets into Parliament, we feel that to the last 'to love what is great, to try to reach it, and then to fail,' has been Dorothea's lot. As Ladislaw's wife she bore children, and her home was a happy one; yet the authoress makes us feel that this was not enough. At the beginning of her career her 'great feelings had resulted in error, her great faith in illusion,' and the most that George Eliot is at last able to say of her is that 'her finely-touched spirit had still its fine issues, though they were not widely visible. Her full nature, like that river of which Alexander broke the strength, spent itself in channels which had no great name on earth.'. . .

No one can close *Middlemarch* without feeling that he has read a great book. He is impressed, and, perhaps, depressed, by its cruel likeness to life; for George Eliot does not bring in the golden age even at the end of the fourth volume, and nothing happens merely in order that the curtain may fall pleasantly. We have seen how to the last circumstances 'broke the strength' of Dorothea's full nature. Lydgate, who, had the author consulted the properties of romance and the fitness of things, should have married Dorothea, dies before his hair is gray, and Rosamond, who broke down his determination to do good work in the world, and made his life ignoble, finds what she calls 'her reward' in a rich second husband. The sober happiness and length of humdrum days accorded to Fred and Mary scarcely lighten the general gray of a sky which novelists usually make it a point of honour to flood with sunshine at the final hour. . . .   [FREDERICK NAPIER BROOME]

The Galaxy, March 1873

. . . Our dissatisfaction here is provoked in a great measure by the insubstantial character of the hero. The figure of Will Ladislaw is a beautiful attempt, with many finely-completed points; but on the whole it seems to us a failure. It is the only eminent failure in the book, and its defects are therefore the more striking. It lacks sharpness of outline and depth of color; we have not found ourselves believing in Ladislaw as we believe in Dorothea, in Mary Garth, in Rosamond, in Lydgate, in Mr. Brooke and Mr. Casaubon. He is meant, indeed, to be a light creature (with a large capacity for gravity, for he finally gets into Parliament), and a light creature certainly should not be heavily drawn. The author, who is evidently very fond of him, has found for him here and there some charming and eloquent touches; but in spite of these he remains vague and impalpable to the end. He is, we may say, the one figure which a masculine intellect of the same power as George Eliot's would not have conceived with the same complacency; he is, in short, roughly speaking, a woman's man. It strikes us as an oddity in the author's scheme that she should have chosen just this figure of Ladislaw as the creature in whom Dorothea was to find her spiritual compensations. He is really, after all, not the ideal foil to Mr. Casaubon which her soul must have imperiously demanded, and if the author of the 'Key to all Mythologies' sinned by lack of order, Ladislaw too has not the concentrated fervor essential in the man chosen by so nobly strenuous a heroine. The impression once given that he is a *dilettante* is never properly removed, and there is slender poetic justice in Dorothea's marrying a *dilettante*. . . .

The most perfectly successful passages in the book are perhaps those painful fireside scenes between Lydgate and his miserable little wife. The author's rare psychological penetration is lavished upon this veritably mulish domestic flower. There is nothing more powerfully real than these scenes in all English fiction, and nothing certainly more *intelligent*. Their impressiveness and (as regards Lydgate) their pathos, is deepened by the constantly low key in which they are pitched. It is a tragedy based on unpaid butchers' bills, and the urgent need for small economies. The author has desired to be strictly real and to adhere to the facts of the common lot, and she has given us a powerful version of that typical human drama, the struggles of an ambitious soul with sordid disappointments and vulgar embarrassments. As to her catastrophe we hesitate to pronounce (for Lydgate's ultimate assent to his wife's worldly programme is nothing less than a catastrophe). We almost believe that some terrific explosion would have been more probable than his twenty years of smothered aspiration. Rosamond deserves almost to rank with Tito in *Romola* as a study of a gracefully vicious, or at least of a practically baleful nature. There is one point, however, of which we question the consistency. The author insists on her instincts of coquetry, which seems to us a discordant note. They would have made her better or worse— more generous or more reckless; in either case more manageable. As it is, Rosamond represents, in a measure, the fatality of British decorum. . . .   HENRY JAMES

(Reprinted in *The Future of the Novel*, 1956)

The Westminster Review, January 1882

'George Eliot as a Moral Teacher'

. . . This question of poverty has been dealt with very variously by different writers; we may suppose that each has treated it from the point of view at which it touched most keenly his own nature. With many of the popular writers of the day poverty is represented as being very vulgar or very uncomfortable. It is not admitted that we may live in a simpler way, with fewer appliances for pleasure and ease than others of our own rank, without being ashamed and unhappy; unless indeed we have a deficiency of good taste.

With Thackeray poverty was always mean. He touched its consequences more from the spiritual than the material side, but still he made its influence debasing. He does not tell us, in 'Vanity Fair,' that Emmy's parents, when they lost their fortune, had to sit on horsehair chairs and drink out of cracked cups; but he sours the kindly mother's nature strangely indeed. And we know of nothing sadder in fiction, or more humiliating to human nature, than the picture of Clive's home in 'The Newcomes,' after misfortune had overtaken the household. The horrible temper of the mother-in-law, the mean acquiescence of the silly wife, the weak-spiritedness of the husband himself, form a picture which even the courage of the old colonel fails to redeem. To see a fine nature daily tormented by small insults, because only of the poverty of the family and the angry discontent of the women, is too painful a spectacle. We want to shut our eyes and turn another way.

Dickens, on the other hand, whether he liked poverty himself or not, had a knack of depicting it as the most cheerful and delightful thing in existence. As long as there was abundance of money every one was melancholy, nobody behaved properly; but when once want had looked in at the doorway, provided that he did not actually force an entrance, all the world was as blithe as a lark from morning to night.

To live in a kitchen compels vulgarity in Mrs. Oliphant's novels; it necessitates meanness in Thackeray's; but in Dickens' it is an assurance of joy, honesty, and content. A shining kettle is a more inspiriting sight than any quantity of polished silver; and a man has hard work indeed to reach the highest pitch of excellence if he is not also poor. Are not these views exaggerated or one-sided? Is there not a truer and a nobler picture possible, in which the precise amount of income is a mere incident, not a predominating influence on the lives of men and women?

We find such pictures in Shakespeare and the poets, and if we study carefully the stories of George Eliot we shall find in her also a fine perception of the value of inward over outward things in human life. She hardly touches upon the quality of her heroines'

8

dresses or the number of their servants. If the question of costume comes in at all, it is with a consciousness that Eppie may look as well in her print gown as Nancy Lammeter did years before in her silvery silk. Lesser writers, when they are intending an ultimate triumph to poverty and fine principles, cannot forbear yielding little side tributes to the delights of the opposite position; they will not go back to the flesh-pots of Egypt, but they must describe them, how excellently the flesh was cooked, in what delightfully artistic pots it was served. When Godfrey Cass and his wife visited Eppie and her adopted father, it would have been easy to indulge in a little description of the superiority of Mrs. Cass's dress and manners. Eppie might have been represented as overcome by them at first, although her filial affection for the weaver would have ultimately triumphed. We should have known that she had proved her moral position superior to that of the greater people, but we should have had an uncomfortable consciousness of an outward inferiority at the same time.

Eppie's profound and yet natural simplicity saves her from this humiliation. Having no longing for the actual good things of a sphere above her own, she has no desire for even the outward appearance of them. Her dress, her style of living, the absence of much furniture in her home, do not, for a moment, embarrass her clear mind or suggest the shadow of shame. Why should she blush to be without things that it would be wrong for her to get? Why should she feel discomposed because she had not that polish of speech which she could only have obtained by neglecting her actual duties? She is the right thing in the right place, and it would have shown more idiocy than intelligence to feel remorseful because she would not prove the right thing in another place, which was not hers.

One of the most healthful, because the most natural, pictures of middle-class poverty which literature has given to us is that of the home of the Garths in 'Middlemarch.' It is a sketch which shows to us the probable troubles of such poverty, the want of means to apprentice the boys, the necessity for the girls to leave home, and so on; but false shame has no place there. Mrs. Garth goes on washing-up the breakfast things while the vicar makes his call; and we straightway wonder why we ever thought her occupation less lady-like than crewel work; it does not blunt refinement or debar intelligence. If she had wiped her hands hastily and sat down, hot and discomposed, and tried to look as if she had been doing nothing of the sort, we might indeed have blushed with her, and ought perhaps to have blushed for her. But if the authoress had been clever enough (as this authoress would have been if she had put her talent in harness to the prejudices of her time) we should have sympathized with Mrs. Garth, and might have thought, 'Could not her husband contrive *somehow* to keep a servant to do this work?' and our hot indignation would have gone out to him; we should have said that it was his duty to give up theories and to make money; that a man's highest virtue was to look after the members of his family and to place them in the best possible position. If they begin life by keeping no servant he must strain his faculties to procure them one; if they begin with one he must toil his utmost to secure them two; and so on up all the steps of the arbitrary social scale; and, if we could have had our own way, a good man would have been spoilt; while clever, capable Mrs. Garth would have sat with her hands before her in her front parlour, trying to enjoy the nominal ease which her husband had purchased too dearly. Mr. Garth had his faults, however; and it was a great fault, almost an inexcusable fault in so good a man, to make himself a surety for the good-for-nothing Fred. He had no possible right to endanger the future of his children, in order to oblige a self-indulgent, extravagant, rich man's son. He did not fail in his duty when he preferred good work with little pay to bad work and more money; but he did fail when he could not say 'no' to an unreasonable demand. Good nature is sometimes a criminal form of self-indulgence; it is succumbing to the weakness of a moment; buying ease and approbation on one occasion for ourselves at the cost of terrible trouble and disappointment in the future, which will not fall on ourselves only, but on others also who have a right to expect thoughtful protection from us.

This novel of 'Middlemarch' deals, more than George Eliot's earlier works, with the intricacies of an advanced civilization; and as sad as Dorothea's blind seekings after a finer type of life than was open to her in her limited sphere is the history of Lydgate's failures. The heroes of old time, the men who were stronger than their fellows, are depicted to us struggling against the brute forces of Nature, or warring against avowed adversaries. The heroes of to-day must fight against their friends. Man has, in a great degree, subdued Nature; he has bridged the Atlantic with his steamers, brought far distant lands within speaking distance with his cables; made, as we have often been assured, the fire his servant and the lightning his messenger; but he has become a more complicated animal than his forefather was, and is more dependent on his fellow creatures. It is hard for him to be entirely noble to-day, entirely free to choose the best course; and Lydgate, though he began life from a good starting-point for independence, and was not crippled by narrowness in his desires or prejudices in his judgment, was not likely to keep his freedom long. He had too much scorn of other men and of their influence on his life; and yet it was partly by and through these men that he had to work; he could not be entirely independent, for they were his instruments; he grasped the weapon of intercourse carelessly, like a knife with which he meant to cut his way to knowledge and success; and the blade maimed him, where the handle might have helped. His chosen pursuit lay amongst his fellow men; freedom to carry it out depended in a measure on their approbation; and yet he thought himself at liberty to follow his own ideas entirely; he believed that the clue to his success lay altogether in his single-mindedness. He was single-minded enough to deserve a better fate: but he was practically wrong; even from his own scientific point of view. If he had had to calculate the course of a planet, he would have been too wise to ignore the smaller influences while he gave the full weight to the greater attractions. Yet he left out of the calculation for his own course of life the innumerable small social bodies, highly charged with heavy prejudices, through which he had to move. The one act of his life which, taken singly, maimed him more than any other, was his marriage. A good woman might have helped him in many crises where Rosamond hindered. Dorothea had made the mistake of supposing that the quality of tenderness was not essential in a husband; Lydgate followed it by the error of believing that intellect was not necessary in a wife. It is astonishing how many men, self-indulgent, strongly perceptive of the requirements of their own comfort in other respects, deny themselves the luxury of a household companion who is capable of entering into their ideas and furthering their ambitions. It was not, however, poverty of resource which compelled Lydgate to put up with an inferior wife; it was not that he was without the qualities that would have entitled him to win a noble woman. He married Rosamond solely because he thought that she possessed everything which a man required to find in his wife; he was not blinded by passion so much as led astray by a want of consideration of the ultimate importance of the subject; just as he had been in his

dealings with the Mawmseys and Gambits, the grocers and apothe-
caries of Middlemarch. If any one persists in looking at his intended
goal without regarding the obstacles about his feet, he may easily
break his leg over a wheelbarrow, at a moment when a strong man
would have opposed his progress in vain. . . .

❡ Everyone now agrees that *Middlemarch* is George Eliot's
masterpiece, and perhaps the greatest of all English novels.
Contemporaries realised this too, and it was received everywhere
with praise and even enthusiasm. Its reception might well make
the modern reader—and the modern novelist—sigh for those
spacious days of reviewing. Some of the long, loving notices linger
on almost every character. The *Times* review, for instance (which
is much longer than the extract here included), does this; and if
one might be inclined on reading it to complain that it does not
single out the portrait of Lydgate, we must pause to realise that this
is not because the reviewer does not appreciate it, but because he
appreciates everyone else too appreciates them in detail and with
discrimination. George Eliot had no reason to complain of the
reviews of this book.

If all this makes us nostalgic, it is not necessarily because the
Victorians were better men than us, and certainly not because they
were better critics; our advance in critical sophistication has surely
enabled us to analyse more shrewdly than they did. But they had
the great advantage of not being so busy; when so few novels were
published, a reviewer could read more carefully (the *Spectator* critic
claims to have read *Silas Marner* forty times!), and write at greater
length (the notice of *Middlemarch* in *Blackwood's* ran to 12,000
words).

To check nostalgia, however, we have also included—to show
how bad a nineteenth-century reviewer can get—an extract from
The Standard, by a reviewer who believes that Lydgate hates
Rosamund, and has misread Mr Casaubon's will.

Writing to Richard Holt Hutton on 8 August 1863 (she was
speaking of *Romola*) George Eliot remarked that 'it is the habit of
my imagination to strive after as full a vision of the medium in
which a character moves as of the character itself'. More than any
other English novelist, she deserves to be taken seriously as a

historian: from memory and observation, from incredibly shrewd guessing, and sometimes from reading as well, she shows us with true understanding the social medium in which her stories move. She took this task so seriously in *Middlemarch* that she gave it the sub-title 'A Study of Provincial Life'. She would have been pleased, then, with those critics who praised her analysis and description of society: with *The Times*'s praise of topographical power, for instance, or the comments of *The Saturday Review*. This latter adds one or two critical comments that might have pleased her less, such as the suggestion that 'this Radical writer' shows 'tenderness for the country aristocracy'. It is true enough—or partly true. George Eliot does like Mrs Cadwallader, though the liking is perhaps personal more than social. She is not so harsh towards town society as the reviewer claims, yet it is true that 'admirer as she is of energy, the energy of rising and getting on finds no indulgence at her hand'. But this inconsistency may be a sign of George Eliot's wisdom rather than of her naïvety. The ready assumption that if competition, energy and the survival of the fittest are good in one sphere they must be good in all is a common nineteenth-century assumption, and it leads easily to the harshest kind of social Darwinism. George Eliot, like Dickens and Mrs Gaskell, seems to accept it only fitfully; if this makes them less coherent than Cobden or Samuel Smiles, it also makes them more discriminating.

George Eliot's realism and her gloom continue, with *Middlemarch*, to occupy and upset her critics. The *Times* critic does not blame her for ending with a 'general gray' in her sky, yet he seems to be suppressing a wish that he could, in honesty, urge her to 'flood it with sunshine at the final hour'. *The Spectator* devoted the whole of its review of Book IV to 'The Melancholy of *Middlemarch*', and it is the best of its several notices of the book. This critic allows himself to say that George Eliot makes the world a shade darker than it is. That is what the *Times* critic rightly refrained from saying. For what it means, almost always, is that this novelist makes it a shade darker than other novelists do.

It would not occur to us today to think that George Eliot's gloom toppled over into cynicism. The Victorians had a readier eye and a lower threshold for cynicism, and though not many of

the reviewers find it in *Middlemarch, Blackwood's* felt it necessary
to defend her against the charge. The best discussion of her
melancholy is that by Sidney Colvin, in what is surely the best
review the book received. Colvin's last paragraph is as good as
anything ever written on *Middlemarch*. The questioning, unsatis-
factory impression that the book leaves is not simply (surely he is
right here) the result of her cool gaze and disillusioned insight; it
is the result of her being a committed writer, with moral concerns.
Colvin's conclusion thus leads us to say that we must choose
between the perfection of a purer art, or being left sad and hungry
by that which has all the impurity of the fully human.

   The one character who was singled out by almost every reviewer
was Dorothea. Much of the best criticism of George Eliot (and
most of the worst) is about Dorothea, and this was as true then as
now. How far is Dorothea's disillusion the result of her high ideals,
and how far of her ignorance of life? Was she too noble or too naïve
for the world? (Similar questions can be asked about Maggie, and
about Felix.) Across these questions runs another: are we giving
the same answer as the author? And if not, is this simply a disagreement, or does it mean we must accuse her of a failure of
insight? We saw the same point raised over Tom and Maggie, and
we can see it raised in Colvin's accusation that George Eliot
'makes a pet' of Celia, and is wanting in impartiality in treating
her so much more sympathetically than Rosamund. This is
shrewd but wrong. It is true that George Eliot hates Rosamund
and has a soft spot for Celia, and it is true that they are alike. But
this need not disturb us unless we feel (which we surely don't)
that the partiality or the prejudice is blinding her, is causing her
not to notice resemblances or to play down differences—to mis-
represent, in short, what she has created.

   Similarly in the case of Dorothea: a lot of what passes for
adverse critical comment may simply be the recording of a disagreement between writer and critic about the value of the
Theresa-mentality. Not surprisingly, the critics divided about
what they thought of Dorothea. *The Edinburgh Review* (in a
passage not here included) called her a 'commonplace young
woman', and praised the author for painting her with 'a gentle
irony that may be unwelcome both to earnest believers in female

devotion and to decided advocates for woman's independence'. *The Daily News*, however, appears to be rebuking George Eliot for being too sarcastic to Dorothea: the ethical disagreement can run in both directions. *The Academy* is very close to George Eliot in its attitude: 'her devotion and purity of intention are altogether beautiful', but 'their beauty must always rest on a basis of illusion because there is no right place for their bestowal'. Nobility and naïvety, that is, are much the same. *The Observer* (not included) revealed a very conventional novel-reader's reaction: 'We are happy to say that Dorothea Brooke, though her mind was theoretic, and "yearned by its notion after some lofty conception of the world, and was enamoured of intensity and greatness," is, at the time we are asked to make her acquaintance, both handsome and exceedingly well-formed, and only eighteen years of age. Those qualities are, at any rate, all in her favour, and prevent us from sympathising altogether with Celia. . . .' (*The Observer*, 17 December 1871.)

The Saturday Review, on the other hand, seems at first to be making a much more sophisticated (and typically modern) criticism, that the author is too closely associated with Dorothea and Ladislaw; but by the end it has dropped into mere moralising: 'Nature has done much for him, but duty—by which all the other characters of the story are tested—altogether fails in him.'

The *Edinburgh* critic made a passing reference to 'decided advocates for woman's independence'; and two of the critics here included have something to say about feminism. The *Times* reviewer is anxious—surprisingly anxious—to deny that the story 'involves some special impeachment of the present female lot'. Sidney Colvin, with hesitation, thinks that it does involve just that: he is intelligent and honest over this, and perhaps right in saying that 'prelude and conclusion leave it still ambiguous'. For George Eliot does seem to have begun by toying with such an impeachment, even if only in the indirect form described by Colvin; and she does seem to have dropped it, so as not to qualify Will's status as a hero, or our attitude to Dorothea's love. Colvin came closer to seeing this than the *Times* critic; but the latter's protests suggest that he saw something.

Two passages from George Eliot's letters concerning the reviews of *Middlemarch* are worth quoting: the first because it shows what she looked for in a critic ('the right moral note struck everywhere'), and the second for its assertion that 'there has not, I believe, been one really able review of the book'.

My Dear Mr. Blackwood,

Before your letter came, Mr. Lewes had been expressing to me his satisfaction (and he is very hard to satisfy with articles on me) in the genuineness of judgement, wise moderation, and excellent selection of points, in Maga's review of 'Middlemarch'. I have just now been reading the review myself (Mr. Lewes had meant at first to follow his rule of not allowing me to see what is written about myself) and am pleased to find the right moral note struck everywhere both in remark and quotation. Especially, I am pleased with the writer's sensibility to the pathos in Mr. Casaubon's character and position, and with the discernment he shows about Bulstrode. But it is a perilous matter to approve the praise which is given to our own doings. . . .

[Letter to JOHN BLACKWOOD, 1 December 1872]

. . . From what you say about public criticism, you will understand why Mr. Lewes keeps all reviews of my books away from me. If he reads them himself, he only gives me an occasional quotation which he thinks will cheer me by its exceptional insight. But he has not yet seen the article in the *Revue des deux Mondes* to which you refer. Though 'Middlemarch' seems to have made a deep impression in our own country, and though the critics are as polite and benevolent as possible to me, there has not, I believe, been one really able review of the book in our newspapers and periodicals. And after one has had much experience as a writer, praise, as such, is incapable of stirring any fibre of joy. What one's soul thirsts for is the word which is the reflection of one's own aim and delight in writing —the word which shows that what one meant has been perfectly seized, that the emotion which stirred one in writing is repeated in the mind of the reader. That you should have picked out those exquisite words of Vinet's—'ou l'élégance la plus exquise semble n'être qu'une partie de la vérité'—as representing your judgement about what I have written, is a peculiar comfort to me. It is precisely my ideal—to make matter and form an inseparable truthfulness.   [Letter to CHARLES RITTER, 11 February 1873]

VIII · DANIEL DERONDA

❧ *Daniel Deronda* took longer to write than any of George Eliot's other books. In June 1873 she was visiting synagogues and reading books on Jewish subjects; on 5 November she wrote to Blackwood that she was 'slowly simmering towards another big book'. It simmered a long time before she actually began writing, but by 23 June 1874 she was 'fairly now at her new novel, and that means "going on".' She finished on 8 June 1876. Like *Middlemarch*, it was published in eight parts, this time at monthly intervals (February–September 1876); and once again it was widely reviewed as it came out.

Letter from John Blackwood, 25 May 1875

The Burlington/May 25/75

My Dear Mrs. Lewes

Reading the whole and rereading many parts of the first volume of Daniel Deronda has more than confirmed the admiration and delight with which I wrote and spoke to you after my first happy sitting over your M.S. That first night I really felt like a glutton dallying over his feast and not reading at all with my usual rapid stride.

The first scene in the dreary gorgeous German gambling saloon with the gamblers all looking so like each other about the eyes and mouth is to the life, and poor Gwendolen's 'enraged resistance' is so true. Her want of early associations with home and the very 'stars' a part of it is beautifully touched. Mr. Gascoigne's pleasant easy tone that made the world 'a manageable place of residence' is very fine.

Gwendolen seeing Mrs. Arrowpoint's folly and not perceiving that she was showing her own hand to the old lady is so like a clever young creature. I did not know what a hold the mermaid witch had got of me until I felt inclined to kick Herr Klessmer for his criticism on her singing and I did not forgive him until I saw him with his hat 'on his hair' when a laugh took away all angry feeling. I knew what must happen to Rex but I was very sorry for him when the blow came and her tears afterwards give me a hope that her creator is going to be merciful to the witch. She is a fascinating witch and I shall not be able to help feeling for her if she does get into 'a swamp, satin shoes' and all. She had 'no objections to be adored' and was hardly entitled to the feeling. That is a magnificent illustration of yours about circumstances weighing upon characters such as hers like the weather upon the Harvests.

There is something very impressive in the way that fear froze that wild wilful heart on the sudden fall of the panel and disclosure of that horrid picture.

The glimpse of the little blacksmith who came to the help of Rex is a perfect picture. I know the little rascal as well as if I had been in the habit of giving him sixpences for years.

Ladies' necks like 'leisurely lilies if they took to motion' is a singularly happy idea. I am afraid there are few necks like that but we have all seen some.

Grandcourt is a most original character and he and Deronda promise to be a grand contrast in your picture. Gwendolen takes Grandcourt up admirably about 'pleasures and follies left off' and his sudden fit of numbness when he thinks he is within certain reach of his object is so true to nature.

There is somewhere a passage about false air of daemonic strength in commonplace unregulated people who know not how to direct their force that has made a great impression on me, but if I tried to refer to all the passages that have done that I should never finish my letter, as when they recur to me I turn to the M.S. and pass some time reading them and the context.

You tell the Tale of Deronda's goodness and that of the stray Jewish Maid so straightly and so simply that no feeling of doubt or improbability arises, and I quite agree with Mrs. Meyrick that Miriam's mother must have been good, as 'wheaten bread does not come from naught.' Sir Hugo is always good and his placid reflections upon good birth like those of a man after a good dinner contrast happily with Deronda's sensitive but terrible fears on that subject. That 'grim walled slice of a house' that the Meyricks have is a happy and consoling thought in the midst of the wilderness of grim looking small houses that really constitute London. How often one has looked at them with a kind of shuddering pain as to what life could be to the inhabitants, but you have given an interior that leavens the whole mass.

Again I beg to congratulate you on this most auspicious opening of another immortal work and believe me

always yours truly
John Blackwood

Letter from John Blackwood, 10 November 1875

Strathtyrum/St. Andrews/N.B.
November 10/75

My Dear Mrs. Lewes

I send proof of the first 256 pages of Daniel Deronda and I know not how to express my admiration. The reading in type transcends even the impression the M.S. had left upon me. In print one can turn back so much more easily to re-enjoy the splendid turns of thought, wit, and expression which adorn every page and had hardly been fully appreciated at the first perusal. *Stupendo*, that often misused Italian phrase, could never be so rightly applied as here.

That wicked witch Gwendolen is perfectly irresistible, new and yet so true to nature, like all the other characters. Her running mental reflections after each few words she has said to Grandcourt are like what passes through the mind after each move at a game, and as far as I know a new device in reporting a conversation. A cautious speaker will here learn that his pauses may also give his interlocutor an advantage.

Uncle Gascoigne is a perfect picture and echoes all over with human nature. His wife, daughter, and Rex are charming, and I did feel for Rex in his terrible prostration. That morning ride with Gwen is a picture, and I see you could not resist the wish that they might gallop away and be happy together. The witch will I hope be saved ultimately but you alone must decide.

In the drawing room here my wife, daughter, and nephew have been reading the proofs and the sort of exclamations are 'splendid', 'glorious' etc. Having read so much more of the wondrous tale than they have I am ordered to be reticent in my expression of opinion about the characters but up to this point our agreement is perfect. Mr. Simpson too, who has been reading the proofs in Edinburgh, writes in a perfect ecstasy of praise. That wretch Gwen has evidently taken the veteran bachelor by storm.

The verdict among us all here is that you are fairly outdoing Middlemarch and I need say no more. The finish of every character however briefly touched is perfectly wonderful and I should have liked to have heard Gwen giving the Curate's 'Perdition catch my soul.'. . .

Letter from John Blackwood, 30 November 1875

45 George Street,
Edinburgh
November 30/75

My Dear Mrs. Lewes

You would get proof of all the M.S. we have last week, which brings us to the end of the second volume. I have been reading and rereading and always with increased wonder and admiration. As I read I constantly lean back in my chair to make sure that I am taking in all the beauty of the thought and feeling. It is like inspiration and you may rest assured that you are writing one of the most remarkable Books that ever was produced by man or woman. I know nothing like it. . . .

The Examiner, 29 January 1876

. . . Such a character as Gwendolen is more like one of Ben Jonson's 'humours' than a real human being: she is not a complete being any more than a picture of a landscape is complete that shows us only its own peculiar mountain ridges, watercourses, and woods. 'George Eliot's' characters have not the flexibility and variety which, for example, the author of 'Far from the Madding Crowd,' whose first chapters were mistaken for her work, succeeds in imparting to his men and women. She always grasps and places clearly before the eye the individuality of her characters, but she fails to invest them with those attributes of our common humanity which only the very highest art is able to make us feel running through the strongest of personalities. No amount of mere intellect, however great, can compass that highest achievement of art. 'George Eliot's' genius is marvellous, but it comes short of that. . . .

The Academy, 5 February 1876

The appearance of the first number of *Daniel Deronda* (William Blackwood and Sons) has been looked for the more anxiously because, in spite of the popular impatience of the serial method of publication, the numbers of *Middlemarch* obtained their success *seriatim*. 'The Spoiled Child' is the heroine of the coming romance; its eponymous hero only appears in the first chapter, where he is introduced in the assumption of a silent superiority to the heroine which is not, apparently, intended to have the same peaceable issue as in *Felix Holt*. The story is one of modern life and society. Gwendolen Harleth is a young lady of twenty, beautiful with the *beauté du diable*, but with no more pronounced diabolical propensities than a love of life and luxury and an undefined ambition after some form of superiority or personal ascendancy which should be reconcilable with all the minor good things good society has to offer to brilliant and beautiful girls. In undertaking to represent such a character, and secure attention for the representation, George Eliot is consistent with one of her earliest principles— indifference to the critic saying from his bird's-eye station: 'Not a remarkable specimen; the anatomy and habits of the species have been determined long ago.' George Eliot insists on having the specimen remarked, not because it is rare but because it is real; all the more, indeed, if it is so far from rare that its reality becomes a powerful influence in human life. The representation of this influence of course remains to be developed, and in the meanwhile Gwendolen's individuality is established, like that of Lydgate, by some personal traits that are not commonly supposed to be associated with the general type of character, though a minutely analytical psychology might perhaps show the connexion to have a root in the nature of things. Thus Gwendolen is superstitious, subject to an inexplicable dread of solitude, darkness, and any other physical suggestion of the existence of natural forces inaccessible to the influence of human wills. Again, though possessing all the vanity and coldness of a coquette, 'a certain fierceness of maidenhood' made her object to being directly made love to, and 'the life of passion had begun negatively in her' when a pleasant boy-cousin ventures to offend this instinct; but she has also still enough childish *naïveté* to carry this grievance to her mother, for whom she has a childishly selfish but genuine affection. One or two paragraphs seem to suggest that we are to have in *Daniel Deronda* a treatment (perhaps more full and central than before) of the question presented in some of the writer's other works, namely, by what property of the natural order it comes to pass that the strength of innocent self-regarding desires is a moral snare unless balanced by some sense of external obligation, or in other words, why egotism is a term of reproach, however fascinating its human habitation. Rex (Gwendolen's cousin) has a vague impression, when he wants to go and bury his dejection in the backwoods, 'that he ought to feel—if he had been a better fellow he should have felt—more about his old ties.' In the *Spanish Gypsy* the 'old ties' of hereditary race-feeling are idealised into a symbol of the strongest bond of human fellowship. In *Middlemarch*, on the other hand, it is noticed as a popular error that 'we are most of us brought up to think that the highest motive for not doing a wrong is something irrespective of the beings who suffer the wrong;' and the reason that the severe morality of the *Mill on the Floss* failed to content some critics seems to have been that there also the ultimate sanction by which right doing was enforced appeared to be only the reluctance to give pain to other persons whose desires were not in any way necessarily more moral or exalted than those of the agent. Without wishing the objective vigour of the author's imaginative creations to be clouded by a transparent didactic purpose, her readers may not unnaturally look for an imaged solution of the logical dilemma—If the desires of A are not a trustworthy guide for A's conduct, how can they be a safe moral rule for B; and, conversely, how is A to be more secure in following B's desires than his own? Or, if the strength of moral ties lies rather in their association with the permanent as opposed to the ephemeral experiences of life, than in their association with altruistic as opposed to egoistic impulses, it will still have to be shown—though not of course proved—how and wherein the permanent conditions of life are more respectable than its accidents. Gwendolen is already cast for the *rôle* of demon, but we do not know whether virtue is to be martyred or triumphant—in Rex or in Deronda— or whether George Eliot has yet inclined her ear to the prayer of the novel reader for a 'real hero,' one unveraciously ideal, who may be admired without any sense of moral discipline and who will steer his way through the pitfalls of his imaginary career with a confidence the more inspiriting because would-be imitators of his prowess might always find excuse in the obstinate circumstances of actual life for any failure to follow in his footsteps. There is something hopefully unpractical in his returning Gwendolen's necklace, which she has pawned in a gambling freak at Baden, and the first number leaves the reader's mind in an admirable state of suspense as to the 'Meeting of the Streams' of incident indicated in its introductory and concluding chapters.

The Spectator, 8 April 1876

... Nor could anything be better than the development of Herr Klesmer's character in relation both to Miss Arrowpoint and to poor Gwendolen. Hitherto, 'Daniel Deronda' has had nothing like the proportion of humour in it to which George Eliot has accustomed us, but it is impossible to find truer humour than the scene between the hum-drum Member of Parliament and expectant Peer, who is supposed to be a candidate for Miss Arrowpoint's hand, and the vehement cosmopolitan artist, who rages so furiously under the impression that this clod of a Briton is thought good enough for Miss Arrowpoint on account of his worldly position, while he himself would be held dishonourable even in declaring his love for her. The fierce reply which he makes to Mr. Bult's innocent compliment —that he had too much talent to be a mere musician—is not only most dramatic in the anger which it expresses at the depreciation of his position in life by a rival whom the world regards as so much his superior, and whom he regards as so greatly his inferior, but has just the enthusiasm and grandeur of conception in it which is needful for the purpose of making the reader feel how completely Klesmer is bound, in his subsequent interview with Gwendolen, to measure her aims as well as her hopes, and to warn her from a life to which she is urged, not by any high impulse from within, but by sheer necessity from without:—'"Ah, Sir, you are under some mistake there," said Klesmer, firing up. "No man has too much talent to be a musician. A creative artist is no more a mere musician than a great statesman is a mere politician. We are not ingenious puppets, Sir, who live in a box, and look out on the world only when it is gaping for amusement. We help to rule the nations and make the age as much as any other public men. We count ourselves on level benches with legislators. And a man who speaks effectively through music is compelled to something more difficult than Parliamentary eloquence."' The double contrast thus presented between Klesmer's conception of Art as a great calling, and Gwendolen's conception of Art as a mode of both gaining admiration and gaining a living after her family had lost its independent position, and between Mirah's horror of what is polluting and Gwendolen's ineffectual wish not to burden herself with relations closer than any to which her nature responds, creates a very fine situation, which we trust George Eliot may so work out in her future numbers as to place 'Daniel Deronda,' in spite of some

superficial defects, on, or not far from, the same level with
'Middlemarch.' [R. H. HUTTON]

The Spectator, 10 June 1876

The Hero of 'Daniel Deronda.'

We quite agree as yet with Sir Hugo Mallinger, when, looking 'at
men and society from a liberal-menagerie point of view,' he piques
himself on the difficulty of classifying his adopted (or possibly his
own) son, Daniel Deronda, and describes the young man, to himself
at least, in words like these:—'You see this fine young fellow,—not
such as you see every day, is he?—he belongs to me in a sort of
way: I brought him up from a child, but you would not ticket him
off easily: he has notions of his own, and he's as far as the poles
asunder from what I was at his age.' It *would* be very difficult to
ticket off Daniel Deronda; and it would do a certain amount of
credit to the classifying power of the men of science attached to
the 'Liberal menagerie' if they could give any clear account of
him. And yet it is not for want of study on the part of the great
writer who has chosen him for her hero. He is much the most-
described young gentleman with whom we have ever had to deal
in her stories. We suspect he is still a bit of a problem to the author
herself. She can't study him enough, and almost always leaves us
with the feeling that there was something behind which she wanted
to say of him, and had not been able quite to find the right word
for. No doubt the chief feature of his character is intended to be a
warm sympathy and receptiveness, much enhanced by reflecting
on his own ambiguous position in the world, and by a sense of
wrong diverted by an intense natural generosity into an eager
desire to enter into the sufferings of others, instead of to resent or
revenge his own. Already this high chivalry of nature has found
four objects on which to lavish sympathy,—the poor artist fellow-
student whose studies Deronda helped at the cost of his own chance
of a scholarship; the despairing Jewess, whom he saved from
drowning herself in the Thames; the spoiled girl whom he first saw
gambling at Leubronn, and afterwards finds betrothed, and later,
married to the cold and cruel Grandcourt; and finally, the consumptive Jewish poet, or thinker, or both, who, in his *tête-exaltée*
dreams, fastens on Deronda as the man who may inherit his ideas,
and thus rescue his thoughts from the grave, in which they might
otherwise be buried with him. To struggling art, to hopeless misery,

9

to sin touched with any gleam of remorse or regret, and to the enthusiasm of pure intellectual passion, Deronda is painted as extending with equal readiness his ardent and tender sympathy, and yet as feeling a certain irritation when people look upon him as so purely disinterested that they cannot even impute to him selfish hopes of his own, in connection with any of his chivalric enterprises. Thus Hans Meyrick's mode of regarding Deronda as if he were quite out of the field when speaking of his own love for the pretty Jewess, Mirah Cohen, rouses a deep feeling of annoyance in the chivalric young hero, whose character had hitherto been painted as having almost too conscientious a tolerance for all courses of action which might seem likely to interfere with his own views. But barring this little touch, and, of course, the high morale which makes him turn in disgust from forms of evil in which there is no sign of relenting or remorse, the difficulty of catching the character is the difficulty of getting any distinct impression of wax, or any other substance which takes any mould impressed upon it. It is not easy as yet to see exactly, what he is, on any of the sides on which he is so lavish of his heartfelt sympathy. His views on art are tentative and very defined; his attitude towards the beautiful little Jewess he has saved from drowning is uncertain, and even in carrying out her own wish to discover her mother and brother, he is reluctant and hesitating; his moral help to Gwendolen, in her errors and sins, cordially as it is given, is of the very vaguest character; and whether or not he has any convictions of his own which will prevent him from taking the impress of Mordecai's musings, and attempting to expound and publish them to the world, is as yet as great a question for the reader as it ever could have been for the man himself. George Eliot has rarely spent more pains on any character, but except its disinterestedness, its large receptiveness, and its moral elevation, we find, as yet, little or no individuality in it. We have not been told what Mordecai's ideas are, and of course, therefore, we could not, even in any case,—even if Deronda had been ever so clearly defined,—know whether or not they would have any fascination for him. But we have so little notion of Deronda's own intellectual nature that, as far as we know, he might be accessible to any Neo-Jewish or other theosophic ideas, which had on them a clear impress of moral grandeur, no matter what they were.

And it is the same with his ethical notions. When Gwendolen, smarting under the sense that she had done a great wrong to

Grandcourt's mistress, Mrs. Glasher, in marrying Grandcourt with
the full knowledge of the poor woman's claims and the claims of
her children upon him, appeals to Deronda for help in atoning for
the wrong in any way she may, his counsel is of the vaguest. In a
former conversation, he had told her that 'affection is the broadest
basis of good in life,' and that the objects of all deep affections are
generally not exactly real persons, but 'a mixture, half-persons and
half-ideas,'—by which, we suppose, he meant that idealised persons,—persons regarded in the light of the highest characteristics
they are capable of *suggesting*,—are the true objects of the highest
affection. When afterwards the question is put more directly what
one who has never been 'fond of people,'—as poor Gwendolen
confesses that she never has been, except of her mother,—can do
to atone in any way for a great wrong, Deronda's only advice is
to enlarge her knowledge, and with her knowledge, her sympathy
with the world. 'It is the curse of your life,—forgive me,—of so
many lives, that all passion is spent in a narrow round, for want
of ideas and sympathies to make a larger home for it.' Gwendolen
objects that she is 'frightened at everything,' 'at herself,' and
Deronda replies, 'Turn your fear into a safeguard. Keep your dread
fixed on the idea of increasing that remorse, which is so bitter to
you. Fixed meditation may do a great deal towards defining our
longing or dread. We are not always in a state of strong emotion,
and when we are calm, we can use our memories, and gradually
change the bias of our fear, as we do our tastes. Take your fear as a
safeguard. It is like quickness of hearing. It may make consequences passionately present to you. Try to take hold of your
sensibility, and use it as if it were a faculty, like vision.' Both bits
of advice,—both that as to extending the range of knowledge, and
so of her sympathies, and that as to making her fear of herself and
her own rash acts a new power to appreciate the possible consequences of action,—are certainly good, so far as they go, but they
do strike one as of the nature of the present of a stone to one who
asks for bread. It was not want of knowledge which led Gwendolen
wrong; and even if a fuller sensibility to the consequences would
have kept her right, her want of sensibility was not due to any
deficiency of selfish fears; indeed, the only tangible good that
advice so vague and abstract could do her was, we suspect, the
confidence its earnestness gave her in Deronda's sympathy, and
the tendency it might have, therefore, to put before her mind an
image of a nature,—half-personal, half-ideal, as Deronda himself

had put it,—of a nobler kind than any to which she had accustomed herself. So far as specific moral direction was wanted by her, we fear there was none.

No doubt the noble vagueness and wax-like tentativeness of Deronda's character,—the vagueness and tentativeness which make him shrink from even choosing as yet any profession for himself,—is meant to be specially contrasted with Grandcourt's sterile, inert, and stony selfishness of imagination, and to suggest to the reader that there is something absolutely good in the plastic moral temperament, and absolutely evil in the impenetrability which shuts out with a sort of rigid snap all purposes but its own. In the fourth book, George Eliot has given us one of her subtlest sketches of Grandcourt, in his inert musings:—

'He spent the evening in the solitude of the smaller drawing-room, where, with various new publications on the table, of the kind a gentleman may like to have at hand without touching, he employed himself (as a philosopher might have done) in sitting meditatively on a sofa and abstaining from literature—political, comic, cynical, or romantic. In this way hours may pass surprisingly soon, without the arduous, invisible chase of philosophy; not from love of thought, but from hatred of effort—from a state of the inward world, something like premature age, where the need for action lapses into a mere image of what has been, is, and may or might be; where impulse is born and dies in a phantasmal world, pausing in rejection even of a shadowy fulfilment. That is a condition which often comes with whitening hair; and sometimes, too, an intense obstinacy and tenacity of rule, like the main trunk of an exorbitant egoism, conspicuous in proportion as the varied susceptibilities of younger years are stripped away.'

All that Grandcourt does, whether in relation to Lush, or to Mrs. Glasher, or to Gwendolen, is illustrative of this tenacious purpose and of this sterility of imagination which accompanies it. His slow and low sentences give all who have to deal with him the sense of 'as absolute a resistance as if their fingers had been pushing at a fast-shut iron door,'—and it is this dull fixity of purpose, as much almost as his utter selfishness, which is brought into contrast with Deronda's wide, and plastic, and ready sympathies. Grandcourt cannot even sympathise with poor Sir Hugo Mallinger's efforts to make the best of his not very fine stud of horses, and remarks that he does not call it riding, 'to sit astride a set of

brutes with every deformity under the sun';—which, indeed, we
suspect Mr. Grandcourt was too much of the conventional gentleman to *say*, under the circumstances, in Sir Hugo's presence,
though he might have said it in his absence. Still, no doubt, the
author attributes this insolent remark to him to make clearer his
absolute incapacity to sympathise with any human being in the
world; and she illustrates the same incapacity in the masterly
sketch of the scene with Mrs. Glasher, as well as in the fine scene
where he forces Gwendolen to wear the diamonds. Deronda, who is
receptive towards every genuine feeling, and especially to every
form of keen suffering, is painted as the very antithesis to Grandcourt, who is receptive only towards impressions which anyhow
affect himself, and in regard to these is quick enough in his perceptions. Of course, the latter is ignoble, cruel, iron-hearted,
generous in nothing but in money-giving where the conventional
feelings of a gentleman are supposed to require it; while the former is
noble, generous, self-sacrificing. But the contrast is meant certainly
to be not simply moral, but intellectual, and we cannot help fancy-
ing that the drift and suggestion of the story are,—that plasticity
and receptiveness of nature are the root of the higher temper, while
sterility, rigidity and impenetrability of nature are the root of the
lower temper. However that may be, it is certain that Grandcourt,
though his insolence impresses us as exaggerated,—and affects us
more as the insolence of a bad woman, than as the insolence of a
bad man,—is much the more definite picture of the two; and that
Daniel Deronda runs the risk of appearing to the end as little more
than a wreath of moral mist,—a mere tentative, or rather group of
tentatives, in character-conceiving, which the author may find it
exceedingly difficult to crystallise into a distinct form. Is not this
to some extent the result indeed of George Eliot's philosophy,
which has parted with all the old lines of principle, except the
keen sympathy with every noble sentiment which she always
betrays, and imported nothing new and definite in their places,
except the vaguest hopes and aspirations? We do not think that
the higher class of characters, though they may well *begin* like
Daniel Deronda's, can ever ripen into any high type, without far
more power of rejecting the multiplied solicitings of all sorts of
sympathies, and far more also of definite conviction, than anything
we have as yet seen in the picture of her new hero. Possibly, however, Mordecai's teaching is intended to crystallise the young man's
mind into clear and vigorous purpose; and we shall be eager to

withdraw anything depreciatory in the present criticism, if that
result should be achieved.   [R. H. HUTTON]

The Spectator, 29 July 1876

The Strong Side of 'Daniel Deronda.'

There can be no doubt that in some, perhaps in many, respects,
'Daniel Deronda' is a much less powerful book than 'Middlemarch,' but in one respect certainly it is more so. To our minds,
the deficiency in power is chiefly to be seen in the incidental
remarks, the observations on life and character, which are always
sprinkled thick through George Eliot's stories, and which were wont
to have so much wisdom, or at least knowledge of life, in them,
that the more you read them, the more they struck you. In the new
story, which is now but one number short of completion, there has
seemed to us a vast deal more of effort and a vast deal less of
fruitful wisdom in the incidental remarks, which have been at once
less easy to apprehend, and when apprehended, less worth the
labour of apprehending. Nor do we think that it is now hasty to
say that, fine as in many respects, the conception of Mordecai, the
prophetic Jew, is, it is a conception which could not well have been,
and certainly has not been, so worked out within the limits of this
story as to justify the introduction of such a character into a work
of fiction. The most inadequate part of the book has been the part
in which Mordecai has canvassed his politico-religious enterprise,
and tried to demonstrate that the Jewish nation might still have a
national work to do in the world in interpreting to the East the
wisdom of the West, as modified by the higher conceptions of the
Jewish faith. But the greatest fault of the book has been very close,
at least, to its greatest secret of power,—a kind of power in which
no previous book of George Eliot's has been nearly so rich as this.
If the conception of Mordecai's religious and political mission has
transgressed the bounds of what even George Eliot can accomplish
in fiction, there is yet a religious element in the story far surpassing
in power and in the skill with which it is developed, anything
corresponding to it in any other of her books. We refer to the very
great power with which the over-ruling influence of a spirit which
moulds human wilfulness to its higher purposes is brought out, in
the story both of Gwendolen and of Daniel Deronda and his
ancestors, not only without any interference with the naturalness
of the story, but even with very great advantage to the connection

of its incidents and the unity of its effect. Indeed, whatever may be the faults of this last work of George Eliot's, we do not think that any of her books, not even 'Adam Bede,' has been so powerfully constructed in point of plot. And it is precisely because the shadow of a higher conception has been thrown over the plot, because the various lives, and the various parts of lives in this book, have been conceived and determined in relation to the demands of a purpose which, so far from being defeated by the resistance of human wilfulness, finds in these caprices the opportunity of effecting something even larger and higher than, apart from that resistance, might have been possible, that we read the whole with so intense an interest, and find both a naturalness and grandeur in the threading-together of the successive generations and the individual lives brought before us, which very few stories of any author's have seemed to contain, and which certainly none of George Eliot's have ever before aimed at in any high degree.

There is in this tale more of moral presentiment, more of moral providence, and more of moral subordination to purposes higher and wider than that of any one generation's life, than in any previous story of this author's, and the effect certainly has been to weld the whole together, in a way that is very unusual with her brilliant but somewhat loosely-knitted sketches of character. Nothing can be finer, now we have seen the issue of Gwendolen's wicked self-will in the number just published, than the connection between her girlish dread of the supernatural—the horror with which the white dead face from which a figure is fleeing in horror in the old panel-picture, struck her—and the destiny which she works out for herself, by her selfish persistence in a course which she knew to be both opposed to all pure womanly instincts, and treacherous to one to whom she had pledged her faith. And perhaps the finest part of this fine picture is the careful, subtle moderation with which it is worked out. Gwendolen, after all, realises the fate of which she had had so dim and dreadful a presentiment, only in a very modified form. While, in one sense, she has been offending more and more consciously against her sense of right, it has been partly because the sense of right itself has been growing in her even faster perhaps than the evil will which has outraged it; so that when at last she finds herself fleeing from the silent accusation of a dead face, the accusation it brings against her is not so fearful as it might have been, and is more likely to bear fruit in humility and penitence than in the mad horror of inexpiable remorse. Whatever we may think, too, of the character of Daniel Deronda,—and to us it remains at the end what it was from the beginning, far too much of an elaborate study and too little of a vivid picture,—no one can deny that the power of the personal influence which passes from his into Gwendolen's life is very finely portrayed, and that the mode in which his evident nobility of nature becomes to her, as it were, a sort of moral inspiration, and a living standard of inward obligation, is very finely conceived and executed. But after all, it is the working-out of the retribution which her sin brings upon her, and the growing of the hatred of the sin, even while the very life of it seems to be growing, too, in her, which is the finest thing in her story. Her interviews with Deronda, after she has faced the fulfilment of her dread, her terror lest he should think her guilt too deep to be expiated, and his fear lest, in trying to give her nature the support it needed, he should be accepting for himself a burden greater than he could support, are all painted in a mood higher than even with this author we were prepared for. And it is curious to notice that, in this last and finest part of her tale, the vein of cynical, and sometimes almost flippant observation, in which she had so often indulged before, almost wholly disappears. She rises to the dignity of tragedy when she passes into the tragic scenes.

And to our minds, the conception of Deronda's mother, of her hatred of her lot as a Jewess, of her inability to resist the iron will of her father, and yet her determination somehow to escape its galling and oppressive yoke; of her apparent conquest over destiny, her career as a great singer, her desire for bringing up her son without the taint of the Jew upon him, and the collapse of her whole resolve as age and disease come on, beneath the inward spell exerted over her conscience by her dead father's imperious fidelity to duty, is still more finely painted. You see the physique of the great singer and actress in all she says and does. You see that she is what she calls herself, an unloving woman, to whom high dogmatic conscientiousness seems a gadfly which pursues us in our madness, rather than one of the noblest of human attributes; and yet you see, too, that she recognises, most reluctantly and grudgingly, but still recognises, the nobility of the ideas which dominated her father's life, and that she acquiesces (though unwillingly) in the duty of giving them a chance with her son. And the author's evident intention to hint that Deronda, instead of losing by his mother's faithfulness to her father's will, had gained greatly by it in capacity to become precisely what that father had fondly hoped him to be, a new leader for his people, a leader with wider conceptions of what lay outside his race's nature and deeper conceptions of what lay inside it, is a nobler indication of her faith in a power which consciously overrules human errors for its own higher purposes, than any we can recall in any of her other works.

If we may judge by the story of 'Daniel Deronda,' George Eliot has real faith in a power which anticipates the end from the beginning, and moulds our nature so as to fit it for a life above nature,—a faith which is the condition not merely of finding any true significance in art, but of seeing any perennial interest in the vicissitudes of history and that 'web of human things' which make up human life. What has been mostly wanting in George Eliot's books is this faith in the larger purpose which moulds men into something higher than anything into which they could mould themselves. And now that it is powerfully presented in one of her stories, though a story in which some of the elements of her genius are less visible than before, it certainly lends to her writing a force and a unity and a grandeur of effect which make up for many faults of execution, and even for occasional evidences of that weariness, which, more than anything in a great writer's works, excites the solicitude and the regret of the reader.

[R. H. HUTTON]

The Examiner, 2 September 1876

It seems as if George Eliot had feared lest the baser tendencies of the age should take heart and flourish from the discomfiture of the unworldly aspirations of Dorothea and the ridiculous collapse of the ambitions of Casaubon, and had resolved to concoct an antidote in the careers of Gwendolen and Mordecai to show the danger which sometimes attends calculating selfishness and light-headed conceit, and the sweet reward which sometimes waits upon disinterested enthusiasm. There must be hundreds of girls more or less like Gwendolen among George Eliot's readers, and the exposure of her shallow frivolous aims is meant to make them ashamed of themselves, and to lift them into a higher conception of their duties and destinies. Perhaps if George Eliot had thought fit to make this lesson to the girls of the period more than a gentle hint, she ought to have increased Gwendolen's punishment, for after all Gwendolen comes very comfortably out of her troubles, being left with two thousand a-year and a developed conscience, and free to marry, if she chooses, a hearty handsome young cousin, whose addresses she had slighted in her unregenerate days. But then Gwendolen's crime, after all, was girlish giddiness and thoughtlessness, and the justice of the circulating library is completely satisfied if her heart is softened, and her wicked husband is drowned. If Grandcourt had turned up again, or if he had left her as poor as she was when she came to him, her fate would perhaps have been a more terrible warning, but it would have been too miserable; besides that, if she had been left in physical misery, we could not have had the same assurance of the reality of her moral regeneration.

The Academy, 9 September 1876

Independently of its interest as a mere story and as a vehicle for reflections, *Daniel Deronda* is eminently interesting, because it presents in a fresh and brilliant light the merits as well as the faults of its writer—merits and faults which are here sharply accentuated, and are not, as is too frequently the case, blurred and confused by the wearing of the plate. Both classes of peculiarities should be by this time pretty well known to the student of English letters. On the one hand, we are prepared to find, and we do find, an extraordinarily sustained and competent grasp of certain phases of character; a capacity of rendering minute effects of light and shade, attitudes, transient moods of mind, complex feelings and the like, which is simply unparalleled in any other prose writer; an aptitude for minting sharply ethical maxims; and a wonderful sympathy with humanity, so far, at least, as it is congenial to the writer. On the wrong side of the account must be placed a tendency to talk about personages instead of allowing them to develop themselves, a somewhat lavish profusion of sententious utterance, a preference for technical terms in lieu of the common dialect which is the fitter language of the novelist, and a proneness to rank certain debateable positions and one-sided points of view among the truths to which it is safe to demand universal assent. To this black list must be added some decided faults in style. In discussing a book which is in everybody's hands, it will be well to show how the above points are brought out, and how they affect the general merit of the book, rather than to indulge in superfluous description of the plot.

In the matter of character, then, we find two signal triumphs of portraiture. The part of Gwendolen Harleth is throughout an overwhelming success: and the minutest and least friendly exami-

nation will hardly discover a false note or a dropped stitch. Her
self-willed youth; the curious counterfeit of superiority in intellect
and character, which her self-confidence and her ignorance of
control temporarily give her; her instant surrender at the touch of
material discomfort; the collapse of her confidence in the presence
of a stronger spirit; the helpless outbursts of self-pity, of rage, of
supplication, which follow that collapse; the struggle between
blind hatred and almost equally blind glimmerings of conscience;
the torrent of remorse and final prostration of will—are all imagined
with a firmness, and succeed each other with an undoubted right of
sequence, which cannot but command admiration. The husband is
almost equally admirable; indeeed, one's admiration is here
increased by the perception that the hand which is so faithful is
distinctly unfriendly, and that the author would like us to detest
Grandcourt. Yet there is not the slightest exaggeration in the
portrait, as he appears before us, acting with strict politeness to his
wife, in no way violent towards her (if we except the occasional use
of somewhat forcible language), and employing, for the purposes of
his refined tyranny, nothing stronger than the methods of 'awful
rule and right supremacy.' If he should appear to anyone all the
more detestable, it may be suggested that it is difficult for any
husband to extricate himself handsomely from the position of
being hated by his wife and having that hatred confided to a
bewitching rival.

The more study we give to these wonderful creations the better
we like them, and an additional interest is imparted by the discovery that Gwendolen is at heart a counterfoil of Dorothea,
animated by an undisciplined egotism instead of an undisciplined
altruism, and by the fanaticism of enjoyment instead of the
fanaticism of sympathy. It might even suggest itself to a sym-
metrical imagination that the soul of Casaubon clothed with the
circumstances and temperament of a fine gentleman would animate
just such a personage as Grandcourt. But these are fancies. The
point of present importance is that the interest of the story
undoubtedly tends to centre in these two admirable characters
and is unfortunately not allowed to do so. Of the third (according
to the author's design, the first) personage we cannot speak as we
have just spoken. The blameless young man of faultless feature
who clutches his coat-collar continually; who at the age of some
twenty years wished 'to get rid of a merely English attitude in
studies;' who, in the words of his best friend, was disposed 'to

take an antediluvian point of view lest he should do injustice to
the megatherium;' of whom it was impossible to believe, in the
still more graphic words of the friend's sister, 'that he had a tailor's
bill and used boot-hooks;' who never does a wicked thing, and
never says one that is not priggish—is a person so intolerably
dreadful that we not only dislike, but refuse to admit him as
possible. Only once, perhaps, is he human—when he persuades
himself on all sorts of ethico-physico-historical grounds that he
should like to be a Jew, solely because (as that very sensible woman
his mother, the Princess, discovers at once) he wishes to marry a
fascinating Jewess. We cannot accept as an excuse for the selection
of this 'faultless monster' as hero the pleas put forward in the
book that it is only the 'average man' and the 'dull man' that will
not understand him, and that the average man is not very clear
about the 'structure of his own retina,' and the dull man's 'dulness
subsists, notwithstanding his lack of belief in it.' In the first place,
the cases are not parallel: for, though the average man may know
very little about the structure of his retina, he can tell a real eye
from a glass one well enough. And, in the second place, the dull
man may fairly retort, 'If you are a great novelist, *make* me believe
in your characters.'

In this dearth, or rather distortion, of central interest, the minor
characters do not help us much. They are far less individual, and
far less elaborate than is usual with George Eliot. *Daniel Deronda*
does not supply a fifth to join the noble quartette of Mdmes. Holt
and Cadwallader, Poyser and Glegg. Sir Hugo Mallinger, with Hans
Meyrick and his sister Mab, makes a shift to fill up the gap, but it is
but a shift. Lapidoth, the unwelcome father, is chiefly welcome to
us, the readers, because of the happy boldness of the incident which
finally unites the lovers. Mordecai we must not, we suppose, call a
minor character, but of him more hereafter.

There is no lack in these volumes of the exquisite cabinet pictures to which George Eliot has accustomed us. The account of
Gwendolen's 'grounds of confidence;' the charming etching of the
waggon passing Pennicote Rectory; the scene of the first ride with
Grandcourt; Gwendolen, after Klesmer has crushed her hopes of
artistic success, and again immediately before she at last accepts
her lover; the wonderful sketch of Grandcourt 'sitting meditatively
on a sofa and abstaining from literature;' Deronda in the synagogue; the stables at the Abbey; the waiting at Genoa for the
Princess; and lastly, Gwendolen's retrospect of Offendene—are all

effects of the finest in this kind. But this good gift and other good
gifts have been somewhat repressed, as it seems to us, in order that
certain tendencies not so excellent in themselves, and very much
the reverse of excellent when inordinately indulged might have
freer play. No one can read *Daniel Deronda* without perceiving and
regretting the singular way in which the characters are incessantly
pushed back in order that the author may talk about them and
about everything in heaven and earth while the action stands still.
Very sparingly used this practice is not ineffective, but the unsparing use of it is certainly bad, especially when we consider in
what kind of language these parabases or excursus are expressed.
We cannot away (in a novel) with 'emotive memory' and 'dynamic
quality,' with 'hymning of cancerous vices' and 'keenly perceptive
sympathetic emotiveness,' with 'coercive types' and 'spiritual
perpetuation,' still less with hundreds of phrases less quotable
because bulkier. No doubt many of these expressions are appropriate enough, and they are all more or less intelligible to decently-
educated people. No doubt the truths of science, mental and
physical, are here, as elsewhere in our author's works, rendered
with astonishing correctness and facility. But it appears to us that
the technical language of psychology is as much out of place in
prose fiction as illustration of its facts is appropriate. In philosophy,
in politics, in religion, in art, a novelist, when he speaks in his own
person, should have no opinion, should be of no sect, should indulge
in no *argot*.

If we are dissatisfied with the Jewish episode which is so remarkable in this book, it is not merely because it has supplied temptations to indulge in psychological disquisition. We do not in the
slightest degree feel 'imperfect sympathy' with Jews, and we hold
that Shylock had the best of the argument. But the question here is
whether the phase of Judaism now exhibited, the mystical enthusiasm for race and nation, has sufficient connexion with broad
human feeling to be stuff for prose fiction to handle. We think that
it has not, and we are not to be converted by references to the
'average man.' The average man has never experienced the passion
of Hamlet, of Othello, or of Lear; he is not capable of the chivalry
of Esmond, of the devotion of Des Grieux, of the charity of the
Vicar of Wakefield. But he has experienced, and he is capable of,
something of which all these sublime instances are merely exalted
forms. Now the 'Samothracian mysteries of bottled moonshine'
(to borrow a phrase from *Alton Locke*) into which Mordecai initiates

Deronda are not thus connected with anything broadly human. They are not only 'will-worship,' but they have a provincial character which excludes fellow feeling. Poetry could legitimately treat them; indeed, many of Mordecai's traits may be recognised,—as we think, more happily placed—in the Sephardo of *The Spanish Gypsy*. They are, no doubt, interesting historically; they throw light on the character and aspirations of a curious people, and supply an admirable subject for a scientific monograph. But for all this they are not the stuff of which the main interest or even a prominent interest, or anything but a very carefully reduced side interest, of prose novels should be wrought. It is hardly necessary to say that this dissatisfaction with the manner and scale of his appearances does not blind us to the skill applied in the construction of Mordecai. Probably no other living writer is capable of the patient care with which these intricate and unfamiliar paths are followed; certainly no other is master of the pathos which half reconciles the reluctant critic. If the thing was to be done, it could hardly have been done better, assuredly it could not have been done with greater cunning of analysis or in a manner more suggestive.

We should have no right to complain that to the simplicity and passion which characterise the subjects and situations of the author's earlier books there has succeeded something more complex and analytic in the present: it is a time-honoured transition, and one which has before now yielded excellent results. But in reality the transition is not in this case great, because the subject-matter really remains the same although there may be somewhat less directness of treatment. The book is little more than a fresh variation on the theme which has informed so much of George Eliot's work, which lurks even in the *Scenes of Clerical Life*, which is hardly in abeyance in *Adam Bede*, which is the professed motive of *The Mill on the Floss*, of *The Spanish Gypsy*, and of *Romola*, which gives charm to the slightness of *Silas Marner*—to wit, the excellence of obeying the instigations of kinship and duty rather than the opposing instinct, 'All for Love and the World well Lost.' Perhaps the motive has hardly depth and volume enough to bear such constant application. But this is matter of opinion. The matter of fact remains, that we have once more presented to us in the contrast between Gwendolen's misery and the prosperity of the sleek Deronda the same moral as we had in Hetty's catastrophe, in the fate which punished Maggie Tulliver's partial declension from the standard, in the ruin and disgrace that sprang from Duke Silva's passion, in the degradation and death of Tito Melema; the same theories which led to the sympathetic selection of Felix Holt for a hero and of Dorothea Brooke for a heroine. The moral, and the standard, and the theories are doubtless of a fine severity, and deal deserved rebuke to the lax pleasure-seeking which has been considered a vice at all times, and is not openly considered a virtue even yet. In the illustrations of these doctrines the author has again given us admirable portraits, and much exquisitely-drawn surrounding. But perhaps she has also once more illustrated the immutable law that no perfect novel can ever be written in designed illustration of a theory, whether moral or immoral, and that art, like Atticus and the Turk, will bear no rival near the throne.

GEORGE SAINTSBURY

The Saturday Review, 16 September 1876

The reader, in closing the last book of *Daniel Deronda*, can hardly be certain to what cause is due the impression that the present work is a falling off from *Adam Bede*, and *Middlemarch*, and a whole train of favourites. He knows very distinctly what his feeling in the matter is, but he has to ask himself whether the conviction that the author has fallen below her usual height is owing to any failure of power in herself, or to the utter want of sympathy which exists between her and her readers in the motive and leading idea of her story. This is a question which can hardly be settled. Some resolute admirers may indeed endeavour to adjust their sympathies to this supreme effort, but there can be no class of sympathizers. Jew and Christian must feel equally at fault; and those who are neither one nor the other are very unlikely to throw themselves with any fervour into the mazes of Mordecai's mystic utterances. Yet we recognize George Eliot's distinctive excellences all through; we never detect a flat or trivial mood of mind; if anything, the style is more weighty and pregnant than ever, we may even say loaded with thought. Nobody can resort to the time-honoured criticism that the work would have been better for more pains, for labour and care are conspicuous throughout, and labour and care which always produce suitable fruit; but the fact is that the reader never—or so rarely as not to affect his general posture of mind—feels at home. The author is ever driving at something foreign to his habits of thought. The leading persons—

those with whom her sympathies lie—are guided by interests and motives with which he has never come in contact, and seem to his perception to belong to the stage once tersely described as peopled by 'such characters as were never seen, conversing in a language which was never heard, upon topics which will never arise in the commerce of mankind.'

And not only are these personages outside our interests, but the author seems to go out with them into a world completely foreign to us. What can be the design of this ostentatious separation from the universal instinct of Christendom, this subsidence into Jewish hopes and aims? We are perpetually called away from the action of the persons of the drama to investigate the motive for such a choice of theme. It might be explained if it were the work of a convert, but *Daniel Deronda* may be defined as a religious novel without a religion, and might have been composed in the state of mind attributed to the hero when 'he felt like one who has renounced one creed before embracing another.' We are at sea throughout. Nobody seems to believe in anything in particular. Nobody has any prejudices. If it were not for the last page, we should be utterly at a loss to know what is the hero's aim in life, to what purpose he is going to devote it. Nobody expects a novel to contain a religious confession, and the reader of strictest personal faith may pass over latitude in this matter in an author whose legitimate work of delineating human nature is well executed; but when a young man of English training and Eton and University education, and, up to manhood, of assumed English birth, so obliging also as to entertain Christian sympathies, finishes off with his wedding in a Jewish synagogue, on the discovery that his father was a Jew, the most confiding reader leaves off with a sense of bewilderment and affront—so much does definite action affect the imagination, and we will add the temper, more than any implication or expression of mere opinion. It is impossible to ignore differences which lead to such a conclusion. It is true that everything has its turn, and it may perhaps be regarded as significant that the turn of Judaism has come at last; that almost simultaneously with the last book of *Daniel Deronda* there has appeared the first of a series of papers 'On the Liturgy of the Jews, by a Jew,' in a popular contemporary, where, to the uninitiated, the subject seems most curiously incongruous. We gather from it that party spirit runs high between Hebrew Conservatives and Liberals, or the writer would not have exposed to the ridicule of the Gentile world certain portions of the 'Liturgy' recited in the synagogues every Sabbath from the Piyutim; and hence that there may be Jews willing to accept the aid of auxiliaries who regard them, not on the side of their faith, but of their race, which we need not say is the point of sympathy and attraction with the present author.

Force of imagination this writer certainly possesses; but a fertile imagination is not one of her distinctive gifts. To one class of her admirers the stores of her exact memory, treasured by the keenest observation, and set off by a humour especially rare in women, and a power of analysis rare in all writers, have supplied one main charm of her novels. . . .

The present story has no representatives of this class. We recognize no figure as certainly a portrait drawn out of the past. The Jew pawnbroker and his family fill the place of these recollections, but they are clearly a study of more recent date; a study, the reader suspects, made with a purpose, and not from the simple early instinct of observation to which we have assumed the others to be due. The failure of one source of supply must necessarily induce more labour. To reproduce, to revivify a cherished memory is a more loving and congenial task than to educe from inner consciousness the personages fitted to illustrate certain views and theories. We feel that the writer's earlier works must have flowed more easily from her pen and been a more invigorating effort than to personify an idea in the person of Mordecai; because, for one reason, the labour of composition, never slight in work of so high a standard as hers, must have been cheered by confidence in the sympathy of her readers, by notes of approval sounding in her ears; but what security of that kind, what echo of wide sympathy, can have encouraged the unwinding of Mordecai's mazy, husky sentences, with their false air of prophecy without foretelling anything? She must know her public too well to have allowed herself any delusion here, and must have been fully aware that Mordecai would be caviare to the multitude, an unintelligible idea to all but an inner circle. The mystery lies, not so much in himself, for this readers would not care to unravel, but in the question as to what reason the author can have had for thrusting him on their unwilling attention. The ordinary reader indeed ignores these mystic persons, and in family circles Gwendolen has been as much the heroine—if we may so term the central and most prominent female figure—as if there were no Mirah.

Of course in the design of *Daniel Deronda* we are reminded of the

10

part played by Fedalma in the *Spanish Gipsy*. Fidelity to race
stands with this author as the first of duties and of virtues, nor does
it seem material what the character of the race is. Fedalma feels
her gipsy blood, as soon as she is made aware of her origin, to be as
strong and imperious a chain as his Jewish descent is with
Deronda. In each, race, as linking past and future together, is the
idea of an earthly perpetuity. In obedience to this sentiment, the
one throws over faith and lover and takes ship with her people;
the other, except that he is lucky in a Mirah, follows the same
course, throws over every previous association, and takes ship to
the vague East.

The Saturday Review, 23 September 1876

If we accept the general view of Gwendolen as being the heroine
in *Daniel Deronda*, rather than the ideal Mirah, who is somewhat
monotonous in speech and same in attitude, it must be granted
that never did novelist present the reader with a heroine so little
attractive, one depending so wholly on her beauty for her interest
or for any shreds of his sympathy. What would be his feeling for a
plain woman, however clever—and Gwendolen is clever—so selfish,
so dead to duty and tenderness, so confident and unscrupulous? It
would be one of simple repulsion. It is the author's design to paint
these gross faults in glaring colours. She spares nothing to give point
and life to her portrait of a self-willed, self-indulgent, cold-hearted
young woman. Nevertheless we are not sure that she means to
imprint on the reader's mind quite the impression which is actually
made. Gwendolen fills in *Daniel Deronda* the place of Rosamond in
Middlemarch; but there is all the difference in the eye with which
the derelictions of each are severally viewed. Rosamond's deference
to the world's opinion, and Gwendolen's defiance of it, certainly
constitute a broad seeming distinction. Gwendolen is daring and
reckless, and does her wrong things defiantly, while Rosamond
basks in a sense of general approval; but each is guided 'by the
strong determination to have everything pleasant,' each is alike
firmly set to get what good things she can out of life, let who will
suffer. They each act according to the needs of a nature clamorous
for what it wants. Rosamond is perhaps most consistently selfish,
after the common idea; but there is an intense, enduring strength
of egotism in Gwendolen which is surely not less repulsive.
Gwendolen, however, has this superiority conferred upon her, that

she is not one of the narrow-brained women who through life regard all their own selfish demands as rights. She has a root of conscience in her. But the reader cannot forget that this conscience was never aroused, and to all appearance never would have been aroused, till Deronda's eye rested on her; and he is not willing to see the great moral difference between one outside conscience and another, between being guided by the opinion of society and being guided by the judgment of one extremely attractive person. Rosamond dreads being despised by the world. Gwendolen is always saying to Deronda, 'You despise me,' and is represented as learning to despise herself through his eyes. But interesting young men are not always impersonations of the Law and the Gospel, and the world would be no gainer were Gwendolen's way of deferring to a single conscience invested with such attractive externals, rather than to the aggregate conscience of society, to become the generally accepted rule. As a portrait, however, she is a vivid and finished performance, and it is only because the character does not please that the skill and genius of the painter have not been publicly recognized as the story has slowly unfolded itself. . . .

It is a strong proof of the early possession of certain images in the author's mind that she makes two of her heroines conceal daggers with the design of murder. Our reader will recall the confession of Tina to Mr. Gilfil:—'"You know how wicked I am, then? You know what I meant to do with the dagger?" "Did you mean to kill yourself, Tina?" She shook her head slowly, and then was silent for a long while. At last, looking at him with solemn eyes, she whispered, "To kill *him*."' Tina's was a sudden temptation, Gwendolen's a lingering one, and her analysis of her own sensations is full of tragic force. But this word 'tragic' reminds us of another feature of the present story. It is full of ideas of the stage, and this dagger is surely one of them. All are connected with the stage in some way or another. Mirah is brought up an actress by her father. Gwendolen has a turn for acting, and proposes it as a profession when poverty threatens. Deronda's Jewish mother was a lyrical Rachel, 'for nine years queen of the stage.' Herr Klesmer, while a musical genius in his own person, is a theatrical critic and judge. Performance, conscious or unconscious, is held constantly before the reader's mind. To be an artist is to make the most of this life—even perhaps, on the principle that life is short but art is long, to extend it; for the mysterious Princess, Deronda's mother, disappears from the scene personating 'another life.' 'With the last words she raised her arms till they were bare to the elbow, her brow was contracted in one deep fold, her eyes were closed, her voice was smothered; in her dusky flame-coloured garment she looked like a dreamed visitant from some region of departed mortals.' The author somewhere remarks that the English gentleman objects to looking inspired. His objection, we think, extends also to other people looking inspired after this fashion, which savours strongly of the Victor Hugo French school. . . .

The Atlantic Monthly, December 1876
'Daniel Deronda, A Conversation'

❡ This highly entertaining essay by James is one of the liveliest reviews that any of George Eliot's novels received, at the time or since. There are three speakers: Pulcheria, who hates the book; Theodora, who adores it; and the judicious Constantius, who understands everyone's reactions, and turns some of his phrases with Jamesian elegance. Pulcheria is something like Gwendolen Harleth—the Gwendolen of the beginning of the book: witty, selfish, catty, intelligent. Her favourite novelists are Thackeray and Miss Austen. She finds George Eliot heavy, and is irreverent about Deronda, about morality, about George Eliot's admirers, and about Jews (this last tastes sour nowadays; but the sourness was not in James's intention). Like so many others at the time, she finds George Eliot like George Sand: 'They are both very voluble, both addicted to moralizing and philosophizing *à tout bout de champ*, both inartistic.' Theodora is rather too earnest for even the most enthusiastic admirer of George Eliot nowadays; by some of the remarks he gives her, we can see that James did find George Eliot too heavy, too moral—why else give her an admirer who says indignantly, or half-indignantly, 'She likes Balzac and George Sand and other impure writers'? This takes some of the edge off our agreement when Theodora says, 'A book like *Daniel Deronda* becomes part of one's life; one lives in it, or alongside it.'

Constantius is given most of the gems, and all the insights. He says that 'there is little art in *Deronda*, but I think there is a vast amount of life'. He praises George Eliot's intelligence: 'It has space and air like a fine landscape.' Naturally enough, he prefers the Gwendolen-Grandcourt story to the Jewish part: Grandcourt is a 'consummate representation of the most detestable kind of Englishman—the Englishman who thinks it low to articulate', but the Jewish story 'is at bottom cold'. It did tickle his imagination: 'It is romantic, but it is not vulgar romance; it is finely romantic'; but he insists that it comes not from the spontaneous George Eliot ('what she is by inspiration'), but from the artificial ('what is expected of her'). Constantius is particularly interesting—and mischievously brilliant—on the relation between the two:

> . . . Gwendolen's history is admirably typical—as most things are with George Eliot: it is the very stuff that human life is made of. What is it made of but the discovery by each of us that we are at the best but a rather ridiculous fifth wheel to the coach, after we have sat cracking our whip and believing that we are at least the coachman in person? We think we are the main hoop to the barrel, and we turn out to be but a very incidental splinter in one of the staves. The universe forcing itself with a slow, inexorable pressure into a narrow, complacent, and yet after all extremely sensitive mind, and making it ache with the pain of the process—that is Gwendolen's story. And it becomes completely characteristic in that her supreme perception of the fact that the world is whirring past her is in the disappointment not of a base but of an exalted passion. The very chance to embrace what the author is so fond of calling a 'larger life' seems refused to her. She is punished for being narrow, and she is not allowed a chance to expand. Her finding Deronda pre-engaged to go to the East and stir up the race-feeling of the Jews strikes me as a wonderfully happy invention. The irony of the situation, for poor Gwendolen, is almost grotesque, and it makes one wonder whether the whole heavy structure of the Jewish question in the story was not built up by the author for the express purpose of giving its proper force to this particular stroke.
>
> HENRY JAMES

❡ On its merits, the review deserves a far longer extract than this; but the whole is easily available, since it is printed as an Appendix to *The Great Tradition*, by F. R. Leavis, and we have therefore preferred to use the space for scarcer material.

The Jewish Chronicle, 15 December 1876

Art we all know aims at producing the beautiful. But this need not be its only although it should always be its principal aim. In selecting its subjects for the realisation of its ideal, art will choose such as are fit by skilful treatment to illustrate nature's moral order, either by bringing out the charms of some virtue, noble quality, aspect or situation in life, and thus while impressing, attracting, and pleasing, thereby enhance in the beholder his admiration and affection for what is good and noble; or it will engage in depicting the hideousness of some vice or ignoble feature, and thus cause disgust and even horror for everything that is low and debased. Indeed, the depth of the impression thus produced and the indelibility of the lesson thus conveyed are the triumph of genius and, as we hold, the noblest use which it can make of art. It is indifferent whether the artist chooses colours, marble or words as the materials wherewith to work, or whether his creation is worked out in a single figure or in a group as does the novelist.

It is but natural that Jewish history, character and institutions, opening out as they do a rich mine of the most striking and touching themes, should occasionally have fired the imagination. Among word painters we actually find three of the greatest geniuses of western literature who engaged in depicting Jewish characters. Shakespeare in his *Shylock* evidently aimed at exhibiting the effect which unmerited contempt, racial dislike and religious persecution can produce on a character in its original structure noble, independent and affectionate. Wounded to the quick in the most sensitive part of his nature, in his religion, domestic affection, and property he breathes vengeance, and, being like Job struck down by blow upon blow, has at last crushed out of him all pride and all manliness. On the other hand, the great Scottish Bard endeavoured to show how a frail Jewish maiden amidst the coarsest brutality of which her race was the victim, beaten down like a reed by the tempest howling around her, yet deeply rooted in the ancestral soil and nourished and strengthened by the sap drawn from it, is able to withstand the hurricane violent enough to uproot oak trees. While Lessing, the keen dissector of human nature, depicts a Jew, another Shylock if you choose, who having emptied the cup of suffering to its very dregs purified and refined from all dross by the fiery trials through which he had to pass, has raised himself to the serene height whence he can look down with equanimity on the strife of passions far beneath his feet, whence he can perceive the nothingness for which miserable mortals contend, rack and torture each other, and has learned to discern and love all that is true all that is amiable in them. To this unintentional trilogy by three master minds, each viewing Jewish character and Jewish life in a different aspect, a fourth representation has been added which discloses before the world a new side in the Hebrew which has never before been painted.

George Eliot in *Daniel Deronda* worthily takes her place by the side of those greatest of artists of modern time. What she essays is unique. She gauges the religious depth of the Jew's holiest feelings. She descends into the recesses of his heart, and brings forth the pearls that have lain hidden there. It is no longer the Jew spat upon, trampled under foot, trembling for life, honour and property, and hunted about like a wild beast. It is the Jew dwelling in safety, freed from the ghetto, come into contact with modern civilisation and culture, saturated by it, whose character is powerfully affected by it, and exhibiting the incisive effects produced thereby in his life, sentiments and spiritual being. It was a great and noble task she undertook, and she succeeded. In Deronda's mother we have the type of the class of Jews who despair of the future because borne down not by legal persecution, which no longer exists, but by social ostracism; but by that prejudice which is the inheritance of past ages and handed down from generation to generation, and which does not seem to get weaker; feeding upon those peculiarities and the reflection of those blemishes by which the bigotry of the past has warped the Jewish character; and which like the scars of wounds continue to disfigure and impede movement long after the original wounds have been healed. They are therefore anxious to save their offspring the pangs of the struggle they had to endure themselves, the contumely and the slights they have experienced, and the constant perils in their path by the obstacles put in their way. With habits sufficiently powerful to keep them where they are, yet with convictions not sufficiently strong to influence them to transplant them in the souls of their children, they withdraw them early in life from all associations that might take root in their hearts and voluntarily subject them to agencies that shall effect the estrangement which they have not the courage to undertake themselves. Most of the losses sustained by Jewish ranks at the close of the last and the commencement of the present century were, no doubt, owing to this cause, which, unfortunately, is still at work—aye, even amongst us. Parents who send away their children to Christian schools at a period when the youthful mind is most susceptible of all outward impressions, when habits are formed which will last through life, when the character is moulded which will decide the fate of the man, may perhaps not have the deliberate intention formed by Deronda's mother, but certainly act in her spirit with a result but too often the reverse of that which baffled her scheme.

Here, also, we have in *Lapidoth* a specimen of that reckless levity which, when it has once quitted the safe moorings of the ancestral faith, has wantonly severed all communal ties and all holy associations that might act as a break upon unbridled appetites, drifts and drifts until sucked down by the whirlpool of the most degrading passions; while in the lowly and poetical *Mordecai* we have the ideal of the highest Jewish associations, the noblest outcome of that lofty teaching, those exalted principles which spring from the deepest root of Judaism, even as they form its most fragrant blossoms and sweetest fruit. The juxtaposition of the highest and the lowest—the dark-minded father of the sunny Mira and the ethereal Mordecai not only heighten the contrast and forcibly strike thereby the imagination, but is also of more frequent occurrence in the Jewish than in the general population. For it is remarkable that among the Jewish people oftener than in others the noblest and the meanest specimens, both of physical and spiritual forms, are found in one and the same family.

And now let us stop for a moment and consider the aspirations, to the realization of which Deronda vowed to devote his life. Such an enquiry is the more opportune, when it is instituted at a period pregnant with great events apparently bearing on the subject, when these events attract universal attention, and when these glowing aspirations are depicted by such a master hand as that of George Eliot, and undoubtedly kindle the imaginations, and rouse the feelings of multitudes. Indeed, the very thought that an author occupying such a proud position should have worked out these ideas with such minuteness, force, skill, and lucidity, and should have brought them forward so prominently, and lavished upon them the wealth of her genius, constitute a great event in itself and invest it with a significance which gives them a claim to careful consideration. Her skilful fingers elicit from Mordecai's finely organised mind, strung with heavenly chords, celestial melodies. It is the old prophetic strains which resound. It is Messianic echoes which we hear. Restoration and re-constitution of the Jewish polity, as of old, is the theme. At its very mention the hearts of thousands of Jews will undoubtedly beat high, and it will send a thrill of delight through every fibre of their innermost being.

True, the number of Jews, especially in the West, is not small in whose souls every such wish has become extinct, and who perhaps would even look with dislike upon such a movement. This dislike is deeply rooted in the existing order of things. They that harbour it are too much imbued with the ideas characterising their age and their respective countries, and too much identified with existing social habits and the current trains of thought to have any desire to remove from their atmosphere. And there are, again, other Jews, and these in still larger numbers, throughout the civilised world for whom the personality of the Messiah has melted away into thin air; who have resolved and converted him into the abstract notion of a happy period when general intellectual and moral progress shall bring on the gradual realisation of all those exalted aspirations which floated before the minds of those God-filled men who conveyed their heavenly visions in those lofty strains of poetry recorded by the seers of old and preserved for us to this day. All these classes have been characterised by our author. But these, after all, form only a small minority, in comparison with the multitudes swarming in the northern and eastern Jewish beehives, who cling to the personality of the Redeemer; who associate with his advent their highest hopes, their most sacred aspirations, who expect from his agency the accomplishment of all those marvellous changes to be wrought at the latter end; and whose most fervent yearnings are towards the land of their forefathers. And there are, undoubtedly, thousands of Christians, and these among the devout and religious classes, who profoundly sympathise with these Jewish cravings, and who would be delighted could they promote this consummation.

Macmillan's Magazine, June 1877
'Mordecai: A Protest Against the Critics'
by a Jew

Sephardo. 'Wise books
For half the truths they hold are honoured tombs.'
Spanish Gypsy, p. 205.

The critics have had their say: the recording angels of literature, more sorrowful than angry, have written down *Daniel Deronda* a failure. And there seems to be at least this much of truth in their judgment that one of the parts of which the book is composed has failed to interest or even to reach its audience. For the least obser-

vant reader must have noticed that *Daniel Deronda* is made up of
two almost unconnected parts, either of which can be read without
the other. Every 'book' after the first is divided into two parts,
whose only claim to be included under the same covers is the
common action or inaction of the eponymous hero. One set of
characters and interests centres round the fate and fortunes of
Gwendolen Harleth, and of this part of the book we can surely say
that it has excited as much interest and bitten as deeply into men's
minds as any of the author's previous studies of female character.
... But there is another part of the book with which the English-
speaking public and its literary 'tasters' have failed to sympathise,
and which they have mostly been tempted to omit on reperusal.
The tragedy of Mordecai Cohen's missionary labours, on which the
author has spent immense labour of invention and research, must
be pronounced to have completely failed in reaching and exciting
the interest and sympathy of the ordinary reader. Mr. Bagehot
has told us that the greatest pain man can feel is the pain of a new
idea, and the readers of *Daniel Deronda* have refused painfully to
assimilate the new idea of the Mordecai part of the book. This idea
we take to be that Judaism stands on the same level as Christianity,
perhaps even on a higher level, in point of rationality and capacity
to satisfy the wants of the religious consciousness, 'the hitherto
neglected reality,' to use the author's own words (ii. 292), 'that
Judaism is something still throbbing in human lives, still making
for them the only conceivable vesture of the world.' The difficulty
of accepting this new idea comes out most prominently in the jar
most readers must have felt in the omission of any explanation of
the easy transition of Deronda from the Christianity in which he
was bred to the Judaism in which he had been born.

The present notice proposes to discuss the failure of this un-
successful part, from the standpoint of one for whom this initial
difficulty does not exist, and who has from his childhood seen the
world habited in those Hebrew Old Clothes of which Mr. Carlyle
and others have spoken so slightingly. And the first thing that it is
natural for a Jew to say about *Daniel Deronda* is some expression
of gratitude for the wonderful completeness and accuracy with
which George Eliot has portrayed the Jewish nature. Hitherto the
Jew in English fiction has fared unhappily: being always represented as a monstrosity, most frequently on the side of malevolence
and greed, as in Marlowe's Barabbas and Dickens's Fagin, or
sometimes, as in Dickens's Riah, still more exasperatingly on the

side of impossible benevolence. What we want is truth, not exaggeration, and truth George Eliot has given us with the large justice of the great artist. The gallery of Jewish portraits contained in *Daniel Deronda* gives in a marvellously full and accurate way all the many sides of our complex national character. . . .

But the new idea of which we have spoken is embodied in the person of Mordecai Cohen, the Jew *par excellence* of the book, the embodiment of the inner life of Judaism. The very fact of this recognition of an inner life, not to speak of the grand personality in which she has typified it, entitles George Eliot to the heart-deep gratitude of all Jews; the more so inasmuch as she has hazarded, and at least temporarily lost success for her most elaborated production by endeavouring to battle with the commonplace and conventional ideas about Judaism. The present article aims at striking another blow to convince the English world of the existence in the present day and for all past time of a spiritual life in Judaism. And we can conceive of no better point of defence for the position than the historic probability of the character of Mordecai, which critics have found so mystic, vague, and impossible. . . .

[JOSEPH JACOBS]

Letter to Mrs Harriet Beecher Stowe, 29 October 1876

October 29. 76

Dear Friend

. . . As to the Jewish element in 'Deronda,' I expected from first to last in writing it, that it would create much stronger resistance and even repulsion than it has actually met with. But precisely because I felt that the usual attitude of Christians towards Jews is—I hardly know whether to say more impious or more stupid when viewed in the light of their professed principles, I therefore felt urged to treat Jews with such sympathy and understanding as my nature and knowledge could attain to. Moreover, not only towards the Jews, but towards all oriental peoples with whom we English come in contact, a spirit of arrogance and contemptuous dictatorialness is observable which has become a national disgrace to us. There is nothing I should care more to do, if it were possible, than to rouse the imagination of men and women to a vision of human claims in those races of their fellow-men who most differ from them in customs and beliefs. But towards the Hebrews we western people who have been reared in Christianity, have a peculiar debt and, whether we acknowledge it or not, a peculiar thoroughness of fellowship in religious and moral sentiment. Can anything be more disgusting than to hear people called 'educated' making small jokes about eating ham, and showing themselves empty of any real knowledge as to the relation of their own social and religious life to the history of the people they think themselves witty in insulting? They hardly know that Christ was a Jew. And I find men educated at Rugby supposing that Christ spoke Greek. To my feeling, this deadness to the history which has prepared half our world for us, this inability to find interest in any form of life that is not clad in the same coat-tails and flounces as our own lies very close to the worst kind of irreligion. The best that can be said of it is, that it is a sign of the intellectual narrowness—in plain English, the stupidity, which is still the average mark of our culture.

Yes, I expected more aversion than I have found. But I was happily independent in material things and felt no temptation to accommodate my writing to any standard except that of trying to do my best in what seemed to me most needful to be done, and I sum up with the writer of the Book of Maccabees—'if I have done well, and as befits the subject, it is what I desired, but if I have done ill, it is what I could attain unto.'

Letter to John Blackwood, 3 November 1876

The Priory,/21, North Bank,/Regents Park
November 3. 76

My dear Mr Blackwood
... It will be rather interesting to see what is the sale of Deronda compared with Middlemarch. Miss Helps, who sees a great many people, and makes her one copy a sort of lending library, says that she never observed a case in which the 'opinions of the press' so totally differed from the impression produced on readers. And indeed from what Mr. Lewes tells me of such reviews as he has seen, I should imagine that no reader of the reviews would conceive from them that the book in question had caused the least excitement in the public or had been followed with any unusual interest. Certainly, if I had not very strong private proofs to the contrary I should conclude that my book was a failure and that nobody was grateful for it, though a certain tenderness was accorded to the production as that of an author who had done more tolerable things. But I am saved from concluding that I have exhibited my faculties in a state of decay by very delightful letters from unknown

readers and reported judgments from considerable authorities. A statesman who shall be nameless has said that I first opened to him a vision of Italian life, then of Spanish, and now I have kindled in him a quite new understanding of the Jewish people. This is what I wanted to do—to widen the English vision a little in that direction and let in a little conscience and refinement. I expected to excite more resistance of feeling than I have seen the signs of, but I did what I chose to do—not as well as I should have liked to do it, but as well as I could.

❡ John Blackwood was once again the first critic of *Daniel Deronda*. Blackwood knew that George Eliot had an almost neurotic need for praise and encouragement, so although the gist of what he says is certainly sincere, one can never be sure (with this as with her other books) how far his enraptured singling out of details is spontaneous, and how far it is publisher's tact. He did however say in one of his letters (quoted in the obituary notice that *Blackwood's Magazine* gave to George Eliot), 'There can be no mistake about the merits, and I am not sure whether I express myself sufficiently warmly. But you know that I am not equal to the *abandon* of expression which distinguishes the large-hearted school of critics.'

Blackwood's unqualified praise was not echoed by the critics. The book was well received by most, and enthusiastically by many; but from the first they tended to claim, as critics have continued to claim, that *Daniel Deronda* was two novels, one very good, the other disappointing, even bad. Almost everyone preferred the Gwendolen-Grandcourt story to the Jewish half: and George Eliot, not surprisingly, objected:

. . . I have had some very interesting letters both from Jews and from Christians about Deronda. Part of the scene at the club is translated into Hebrew in a German-Jewish newspaper. On the other hand a Christian (highly accomplished) thanks me for embodying the principles by which Christ wrought and will conquer. This is better than the laudation of readers who cut the book into scraps and talk of nothing in it but Gwendolen. I meant everything in the book to be related to everything else there. . . .

[Letter to MME EUGÈNE BODICHON, 2 October 1876]

... Since we came home at the beginning of September I have been
made aware of much repugnance or else indifference towards the
Jewish part of Deronda, and of some hostile as well as adverse
reviewing. On the other hand there have been the strongest
expressions of interest—some persons adhering to the opinion,
started during the early numbers, that the book is my best—
delighted letters have here and there been sent to me, and the sale
both in America and in England has been an unmistakeable
guarantee that the public has been touched. Words of gratitude
have come from Jews and Jewesses, and there are certain signs that
I may have contributed my mite to a good result.

> [G.E.'s *Journal*, 1 December 1876]

Some of those who objected to the Jewish parts can surely be
accused of prejudice: the critic of *The Saturday Review* has taken
little care to conceal his well-bred anti-Semitism, and it slips out
in several revealing phrases: the 'sense of bewilderment and
affront', the reference to George Eliot's '*subsidence* into Jewish
hopes and aims', the reviewer's amusement at finding 'that party
spirit runs high between Hebrew Conservatives and Liberals'.
George Saintsbury (the critic of *The Academy*), however, is careful
to assure us (and there seems no reason to doubt him) that he feels no
imperfect sympathy with Jews, and holds 'that Shylock had the
best of the argument'. We do not *have* to assume prejudice in a
reader who finds the Jewish part bad: if we did, which of us would
'scape whipping? Yet Jewish critics (and who can put his hand on
his heart and blame them?) did suspect this: 'The greatest pain
man can feel,' wrote the author of 'Mordecai: A Protest against the
Critics' in *Macmillan's Magazine*, 'is the pain of a new idea. . . .
This idea we take to be that Judaism stands on the same level as
Christianity.'

Daniel Deronda was well received by Jews: gratefully, enthusiastically, uncritically. There was even a book published on it:
George Eliot and Judaism: an Attempt to Appreciate Daniel Deronda,
actually a translation of a three-part article by David Kaufmann
in the *Monatschrift für Geschichte und Wissenschaft des Judenthums*
(1877). There is no reason to believe that Kaufmann, or the other
Jewish critics who responded so favourably, were less perceptive or
sensitive than gentile readers: the whole episode shows us, as

neatly as can be, how involvement with a book's subject-matter tends to blind one critically. Perhaps it shows us too that it is better to be blinded, uncritical and warmly alive, than to be cool, shrewd and disdainful.

The Jewish critics were more concerned to relate the book to Jewish life than with its artistry. In his last two paragraphs the reviewer in *The Jewish Chronicle* moves away from the book altogether to advocate what was later to become Zionism; and this article was followed by another, still entitled 'Daniel Deronda', but entirely concerned with the possibility of the 'restoration to Palestine'.

Another general complaint was made of *Daniel Deronda*, as of all George Eliot's later work: that it was over-intellectual. This comes in its simplest form, clearly and (one must admit) sensibly stated, in Saintsbury's *Academy* review: the most he will grant in favour of comment and generalisation by the author is that 'very sparingly used, this practice is not ineffective', and it is almost impossible, from this premise, wholly to approve of George Eliot. The author of 'George Eliot as a Novelist' (*Westminster Review*, 1878; see p. 176) preferred the early novels (as did Trollope: as did many) on the same grounds: she has 'taken thought' in the later books, she is too concerned with 'certain important problems', too learned, or too clever, or too expository, at the expense of the story: 'The object of the novel writer is to tell a story.' The mild purism of these two critics ('on the wrong side of the account must be placed . . . a somewhat lavish profusion of sententious utterance') was common at the time, and for a more sophisticated statement of it we can turn to Henry James: Constantius's objection to the Jewish half of the book is that it is theoretic, not the immediate creation of the story-teller.

The real George Eliot enthusiasts are those who like their novels to smack of something besides literature. This taste is more widespread than literary critics, and Jamesians, always admit: the conventional Blackwood begins his praise of the book by mentioning 'the splendid turns of thought, wit and expression which adorn every page'. Perhaps the reflective, garrulous, tendentious novelists will always command a greater public than the pure artists.

The *Saturday Review* critic who lamented that George Eliot's store of cherished memories had failed, and been replaced by 'labour' was also objecting to over-intellectualism: to 'educe from inner consciousness' is to work more with the intellect and less with a creative spontaneity than if one allowed one's early memories to spill over into one's story. The critic may be partly right in this instance: the minor characters of *Daniel Deronda* have not always the life of Mrs Poyser or Aunt Glegg. It is mere prejudice, however, to believe that no virtues can offset this loss, or that the spontaneous is the only way of creation. George Eliot's intellectualism may not be a weakness at all; and even if it is, it may be a weakness inextricably linked to her strength. The *Spectator* critic is perhaps harsh when he condemns her 'incidental remarks' and 'observations on life and character'; but he is both honest and shrewd when he remarks on the close connexion between this and the book's greatest power—'the shadow of a higher conception'—that holds everything together. It is difficult to be sure just what he means by this, however; and without being sure, it is difficult to agree or disagree. For if this 'shadow of a higher conception' is the construction of the book, the interweaving of theme and plot, the anticipations and the ironies, then it is indeed a sign of George Eliot's genius; but if (as at times appears) it is a sense of providence, a faith in a power (even a Power) which guides and plans, then it neither is nor should be present in the book.

A contemporary reviewer in America (Edward Whipple in the *North American Review*, January 1877) praised George Eliot's intellectual powers without even dreaming they were a literary liability: 'George Eliot might hold, in one corner of her broad brain, all that portion of Scott's intellect which dealt with the philosophy of history as distinguished from its picturesqueness; in another corner, all that part of the intellect of Dickens which, in dealing with political economy, was prone to substitute benevolent sentiments for inexorable laws; and in still another corner, all that portion of the intellect of Thackeray which penetrated beneath the social shams he pitilessly satirized to the principles which make society possible.' He then went on to praise, just as enthusiastically, her wide-ranging sympathies, with no sense of incongruity or incompatibility. And was he wrong?

The moral issues raised by *Daniel Deronda* are, of course, bodied forth as literature, not merely discussed in the abstract; but there is always a moral philosopher's discussion to be held over any great novel, and the *Academy* reviewer of Part I (surely not Saintsbury this time), entering this discussion with a different position from George Eliot's, deserves hearing and answering. His summary of her moral position is fair, and the sentence he quotes ('We are most of us brought up to think that the highest motive for not doing a wrong is something irrespective of the beings who suffer the wrong') is apt. What of the criticism that to set up altruism an an intrinsic good is to ignore intrinsic valuations, and prefer the worst desires of others to our own better desires? George Eliot would surely have read this objection with respect, and considered it worth answering. Readers may care to amuse themselves by constructing her answer.

Naturally enough, the two principal characters, Deronda and Gwendolen, received the most attention. Deronda was found stiff by most critics, though not by all. *The Academy* is interesting here: when its reviewer had read the first part only, he hoped that George Eliot would 'incline her ear to the prayer of the novel reader for a "real hero", one unveraciously ideal who may be admired without any sense of moral discipline'. Moral discipline may not be absent, but in general this is surely what George Eliot did; and readers have not, after all, thanked her for it. *The Spectator* contrasts Deronda with Grandcourt, finding Grandcourt 'the more definite picture of the two', and indicating the limitations of the portrait of Deronda with several happy phrases: 'The difficulty of catching the character is the difficulty of getting any distinct impression of wax'; or (better and briefer) that 'he runs the risk of appearing to the end as little more than a wreath of moral mist'.

Yet several reviewers found that Deronda was not altogether waxlike. Does not the line that separates the quick from the dead in this uneven novel run through Deronda himself: much is shrewd and moving in his relations with Gwendolen. *The Spectator* is worth pondering when after admitting that Deronda is 'far too much of an elaborate study and too little of a vivid picture' it finds that 'the power of the personal influence which passes from his into Gwendolen's life is very finely portrayed'.

11

Gwendolen is perhaps George Eliot's finest single creation; and it is pleasant to record that contemporary critics realised this. Saintsbury speaks for many in finding her an 'overwhelming success'. Perhaps the one interesting deviation here is the *Saturday Review* critic, who in comparing her with Rosamund offers a clear case of the blinding effects of moral concern. George Eliot is clear that Gwendolen was luckier than Rosamund: for her the dictates of conscience and society are embodied in a single person of whom she is in awe, whereas Rosamund had no check on her selfishness save a dread of social censure. Now the greatest of George Eliot's insights is surely this, that such a dread is worth little, since almost total selfishness is quite compatible with conduct that is socially unexceptionable. For the critic to disapprove, as he does, of 'Gwendolen's way of deferring to a single conscience invested with such attractive externals' is to replace insight with moralising. Since George Eliot is so often accused of this, it is gratifying to find an instance where she is less narrow, and less moralistic, than her critic.

We have included two short extracts from the serial notice of the novel in *The Examiner*. The first is to remind ourselves that there is nothing reviewers will not say. If the contrast between individual, three-dimensional characters and 'humours' means anything, then George Eliot creates the former; with James and (perhaps) Thackeray, she seems the very type of the individualising novelist. Yet here is a critic who sees in Gwendolen something like a Jonsonian humour. We can simply conclude that he was imperceptive; and we can also notice that for the Victorians this contrast was evaluative, not merely descriptive. They preferred a novel filled with individuals to a novel built on a moral pattern, and by calling Gwendolen a humour the critic is simply expressing his disappointment with the book.

The paragraph we have quoted from his review of the whole (2 September 1876) is also wrong-headed (did George Eliot have so moralising a purpose?), but this time one can easily forgive it: for his slow, ironic suggestion that Gwendolen does not, after all, do so badly, is the only passage in any of the reviews that reads as if it could have been written by George Eliot herself. And for that one can forgive anything.

IX · GENERAL APPRAISALS

The Atlantic Monthly, October 1866

'The Novels of George Eliot'

... It is very probable that her colours are a little too bright, and her shadows of too mild a gray, that the sky of her landscapes is too sunny, and their atmosphere too redolent of peace and abundance. Local affection may be accountable for half of this excess of brilliancy; the author's native optimism is accountable for the other half.

I do not remember, in all her novels, an instance of gross misery of any kind not directly caused by the folly of the sufferer. There are no pictures of vice or poverty or squalor. There are no rags, no gin, no brutal passions. That average humanity which she favours is very *borné* in intellect, but very genial in heart, as a glance at its representatives in her pages will convince us. In *Adam Bede*, there is Mr. Irwine, the vicar, with avowedly no qualification for his profession, placidly playing chess with his mother, stroking his dogs, and dipping into Greek tragedies; there is the excellent Martin Poyser at the Farm, good-natured and rubicund; there is his wife, somewhat too sharply voluble, but only in behalf of cleanliness and honesty and order; there is Captain Donnithorne at the Hall, who does a poor girl a mortal wrong, but who is, after all, such a nice, good-looking fellow; there are Adam and Seth Bede, the carpenter's sons, the strongest, purest, most discreet of young rustics. The same broad felicity prevails in *The Mill on the Floss*. Mr. Tulliver, indeed, fails in business; but his failure only serves as an offset to the general integrity and prosperity. His son is obstinate and wilful; but it is all on the side of virtue. His daughter is somewhat sentimental and erratic; but she is more conscientious yet. . . .

One word more. Of all the impressions—and they are numerous —which a reperusal of George Eliot's writings has given me, I find the strongest to be this: that (with all deference to *Felix Holt, the Radical*) the author is in morals and aesthetics essentially a conservative. In morals her problems are still the old, passive problems.

I use the word 'old' with all respect. What moves her most is the idea of a conscience harassed by the memory of slighted obligations. Unless in the case of Savonarola, she has made no attempt to depict a conscience taking upon itself great and novel responsibilities. In her last work, assuredly such an attempt was—considering the title—conspicuous by its absence.

Of a corresponding tendency in the second department of her literary character,—or perhaps I should say in a certain middle field where morals and aesthetics move in concert,—it is very difficult to give an example. A tolerably good one is furnished by her inclination to compromise with the old tradition—and here I use the word 'old' *without* respect—which exacts that a serious story of manners shall close with the factitious happiness of a fairy-tale. I know few things more irritating in a literary way than each of her final chapters,—for even in *The Mill on the Floss* there is a fatal 'Conclusion.' Both as an artist and a thinker, in other words, our author is an optimist; and although a conservative is not necessarily an optimist, I think an optimist is pretty likely to be a conservative.   HENRY JAMES

The Contemporary Review, August 1872

When we have passed in review the works of that great writer who calls herself George Eliot, and given for a time our use of sight to her portraitures of men and women, what form, as we move away, persists on the field of vision, and remains the chief centre of interest for the imagination? The form not of Tito, or Maggie, or Dinah, or Silas, but of one who, if not the real George Eliot, is that 'second self' who writes her books, and lives and speaks through them. Such a second self of an author is perhaps more substantial than any mere human personality encumbered with the accidents of flesh and blood and daily living. It stands at some distance from the primary self, and differs considerably from its fellow. It presents its person to us with fewer reserves; it is independent of local and temporary motives of speech or of silence; it knows no man after the flesh; it is more than an individual; it utters secrets, but secrets which all men of all ages are to catch; while, behind it, lurks well pleased the veritable historical self secure from impertinent observation and criticism. With this second self of George Eliot it is, not with the actual historical person, that we have to do. And when, having closed her books, we gaze outward with the mind's eye, the spectacle we see is that most impressive spectacle of a great nature, which has suffered and has now attained, which was perplexed and has now grasped the clue—standing before us not without tokens on lip and brow of the strife and the sufferings, but resolute, and henceforth possessed of something which makes self-mastery possible. The strife is not ended, the pain may still be resurgent; but we perceive on which side victory must lie.

This personal accent in the writings of George Eliot does not interfere with their dramatic truthfulness; it adds to the power with which they grasp the heart and conscience of the reader. We cannot say with confidence of any one of her creations that it is a projection of herself; the lines of their movement are not deflected by hidden powers of attraction or repulsion peculiar to the mind of the author; most noteworthy is her impartiality towards the several creatures of her imagination; she condemns but does not hate; she is cold or indifferent to none; each lives his own life, good or bad; but the author is present in the midst of them, indicating, interpreting; and we discern in the moral laws, the operation of which presides over the action of each story, those abstractions from the common fund of truth which the author has found most needful to her own deepest life. We feel in reading these books that we are in the presence of a soul, and a soul which has had a history. . . .

The same doctrine of the necessity of self-renunciation, of the obligation laid upon men to accept some other rule of conduct than the desire of pleasure is enforced in the way of warning with terrible emphasis. Tito Melema, Arthur Donnithorne, Godfrey Cass, Maggie Tulliver, are in turn assailed by one and the same temptation—to deny or put out of sight our duties to others, to gratify some demand for egoistic pleasure or happiness, or to avoid some wholesome necessary pain. Arthur, vain, affectionate, susceptible, owed no one a grudge, and would have liked to see everyone about him happy, and ready to acknowledge that they owed a great part of their happiness to the handsome young landlord. Tito was clever and beautiful, kind and gentle in his manners, without a thought of anything cruel or base. And Godfrey was full of easy good nature; and Maggie, of a wealth of eager love. But in the linked necessity of evil, each of these, beginning with a soft yielding to egoistic desires, becomes capable of deeds or of wishes that are base and cruel. '"It's a woman," said Silas, speaking low and half-breathlessly, just as Godfrey came up. "She's dead, I think—dead in the snow at the stone-pits, not far from my door." Godfrey felt a great throb: there was one terror in his mind at that moment—it was, that the woman might *not* be dead. That was an evil terror—an ugly inmate to have found a nestling-place in Godfrey's kindly disposition.' Maggie has heard the voice of the great mediæval bearer of the Cross; a higher rule than that of self-pleasing lives in her inner-most conscience, and therefore she has strength at the last to renounce the cruel pursuit of personal joy, and to accept a desert for her feet henceforth to walk in, and bitter waters to allay her thirst.

The scientific observation of man, and in particular the study of the mutual relations of the individual and society, come to rein-force the self-renouncing dictates of the heart. To understand any individual apart from the whole life of the race is impossible. We are the heirs intellectual and moral of the past; there is no such thing as naked manhood; the heart of each of us wears livery which it cannot throw off. Our very bodies differ from those of primeval savages—differ, it may be, from those of extinct apes only by the gradual gains of successive generations of ancestors. Our instincts, physical and mental, our habits of thought and feeling, the main tendency of our activity, these are assigned to us by the common life which has preceded and which surrounds our own. 'There is no private life,' writes George Eliot in 'Felix Holt,' 'which has not been determined by a wider public life, from the time when the primeval milkmaid had to wander with the wanderings of her clan, because the cow she milked was one of a herd which had made the pastures bare.'

If this be so, any attempt to render our individual life indepen-dent of the general life of the past and present, any attempt to erect a system of thought and conduct out of merely personal convictions and personal desires must be a piece of slight, idealistic fatuity. The worship of the Goddess of Reason and the constitution of the year one, are the illusions of revolutionary idealism, and may fitly be transferred from this Old World which has a history to the rising philosophers and politicians of Cloudcuckoo-town. Not Reason alone, but Reason and Tradition in harmonious action guide our path to the discovery of truth:—

> We had not walked
> But for Tradition; we walk evermore
> To higher paths by brightening Reason's lamp.

Do we desire to be strong? We shall be so upon one condition—that we resolve to draw for strength upon the common fund of thought and feeling and instinct stored up, within us and without us, by the race. We enter upon our heritage as soon as we consent to throw in our lot with that of our fellow-men, those who have gone before us, who are now around us, who follow after us, continuing our lives and works. War waged against the powers by which we are encompassed leads to inevitable defeat; our safety, our honour, our greatness lie in an unconditional surrender.

It will be readily seen how this way of thinking abolishes rights, and substitutes duties in their place. Of rights of man, or rights of woman, we never hear speech from George Eliot. But we hear much of the duties of each. The claim asserted by the individual on behalf of this or that disappears, because the individual surrenders his independence to collective humanity, of which he is a part. And it is another consequence of this way of thinking that the leadings of duty are most often looked for, not within, in the promptings of the heart, but without, in the relations of external life, which connect us with our fellow-men. Our great English novelist does not preach as her favourite doctrine the indefeasible right of love to gratify itself at the expense of law; with the correlative right, equally indefeasible, to cast away the marriage bond as soon as it has become a painful incumbrance. She regards the formal contract, even when its spirit has long since died, as sacred and of binding force. Why? Because it is a formal contract. 'The light abandonment of ties, whether inherited or voluntary, because they had ceased to be pleasant, would be the uprooting of social and personal virtue.' Law is sacred. Rebellion, it is true, may be sacred also. There are moments of life 'when the soul must dare to act upon its own warrant, not only without external law to appeal to, but in the face of a law which is not unarmed with Divine lightnings—lightnings that may yet fall if the warrant has been false.' These moments, however, are of rare occurrence, and arise only in extreme necessity. When Maggie and Stephen Guest are together and alone in the Mudport Inn, and Maggie has announced her determination to accompany him no farther, Stephen pleads:— '"We have proved that it was impossible to keep our resolutions. We have proved that the feeling which draws us to each other is too strong to be overcome: that natural law surmounts every other; we can't help what it clashes with." "It is not so, Stephen. I'm quite sure that is wrong. I have tried to think it again and again; but I see, if we judged in that way, there would be a warrant for all treachery and cruelty. We should justify breaking the most sacred ties that can ever be formed on earth. If the past is not to bind us, where can duty lie? We should have no law but the inclination of the moment."' Maggie returns to St. Oggs: Fedalma and Don Silva part: Romola goes back to her husband's house. We can imagine how unintelligible such moral situations, and such moral solutions, would appear to a great female novelist in France. The Saint Clotilda of Positivism had partly written a large work intended to refute the attacks upon marriage contained in the writings of George Sand,' 'to whom,' adds her worshipping colleague, 'she was intellectually no less than morally superior.' Perhaps we may more composedly take on trust the excellence of Madame Clotilde de Vaux's refutation, inasmuch as the same object has been indirectly accomplished by the great female novelist of England, who for her own part has not been insensible to anything that was precious in the influence of Comte.

'If the past is not to bind us, where can duty lie?' As the life of the race lying behind our individual life points out the direction in which alone it can move with dignity and strength, so our own past months and years lying behind the present hour and minute deliver over to these a heritage and a tradition which it is their wisdom joyfully to accept when that is possible. There are moments, indeed, which are the beginning of a new life; when, under a greater influence than that of the irreversible Past, the current of our life takes an unexpected course; when a single act transforms the whole aspect of the world in which we move; when contact with a higher nature than our own suddenly discovers to us some heroic quality of our heart of the existence of which we had not been aware. Such is the virtue of confession of evil deeds or desires to a fellow-man, it restores us to an attitude of noble simplicity; we are rescued from the necessity of joining hands with our baser self. But these moments of new birth do not come by intention or choice. The ideal which we may set before ourselves, and count upon making our own by constancy and fidelity of heart, is that which Don Silva imagines for himself:—

> A Past that lives
> On through an added Present, stretching still
> In hope unchecked by shaming memories
> To life's last breath.

If no natural piety binds our days together, let us die quickly rather than die piecemeal by the slow paralyzing touch of time. All that helps to hold our past and present together is therefore precious and sacred. It is well that our affections should twine tenderly about all material tokens and memorials of bygone days. Why should Tito keep his father's ring? Why indulge a foolish sentiment, a piece of mere superstition, about an inanimate object? And so Tito sells the ring, and with it closes the bargain by which he sells his soul. There is, indeed, a noble pressing forward to things that are before, and forgetting of things that are behind. George Eliot is not attracted to represent a character in which such an ardour is predominant, and the base forgetting of things behind alarms and shocks her. It is noted, as characteristic of Hetty's shallow nature, that in her dream of the future, the brilliant future of the Captain's wife, there mingles no thought of her second parents, no thought of the children she had helped to tend, of any youthful companion, any pet animal, any relic of her own childhood. 'Hetty could have cast all her past life behind her, and never cared to be reminded of it again. I think she had no feeling at all towards the old house, and did not like the Jacob's ladder and the long row of hollyhocks in the garden better than any other flowers—perhaps not so well.' Jubal, after his ardent pursuit of song through the world, would return to Lamech's home, 'hoping to find the former things.' Silas Marner would see once more the town where he was born, and Lantern Yard, where the lots had declared him guilty. But Hetty is like a plant with hardly any roots; 'lay it over your ornamental flower-pot and it blossoms none the worse.'

This is the life we mortals live. And beyond life lies death. *Now* it is not hard to face it. We have already given ourselves up to the large life of our race. We have already died as individual men and women. And we see how the short space of joy, of suffering, and of activity allotted to each of us urges to helpful toil, and makes impossible for us the 'glad idlesse' of the immortal denizen of earth. This is the thought of 'Jubal.' When the great artist returns to his early home, he is already virtually deceased—he has entered into subjective existence. Jubal the maker of the lyre is beaten with the flutes of Jubal's worshippers. This is tragic. His apotheosis and his martyrdom were one. George Eliot is not insensible to the anguish of the sufferer. But a strenuous and holy thought comes to make his death harmonious as his life. He has given his gift to men. He has enriched the world. He is incorporate in

> A strong persistent life
> Panting through generations as one breath,
> And filling with its soul the blank of death.

                                        EDWARD DOWDEN

The Spectator, 12 February 1876

'George Eliot's Heroines'

... She has little interest in women, unless she has *enough* interest either to sympathise with or dislike them.... We may take it almost as a general rule, that when GE paints a woman's character at all, she herself regards it with some very strongly marked feeling, and cannot, therefore, paint it with a light hand....

It is quite true, we suppose, that many of the women of this great novelist will be the delights of English literature as long as the language endures. The spiritual beauty of Dinah, the childish and almost involuntary selfishness and love of ease which give a strange pathos to the tragic fate of Hetty, the vague ardour of Dorothea, the thin amiability, but thorough unlovableness, of Rosamond, all these, and many other feminine paintings by the same hand, will be historic pictures in our literature if human foresight be worth anything, at least as long as Sir Walter Scott's studies of James, and Baby Charles, and Elizabeth, and Mary Stuart and Leicester are regarded as historic pictures in this land. But George Eliot's heroines are certainly never likely to be remarkable for airiness of touch. It is not Sir Joshua Reynolds, but rather Vandyk, or even Rembrandt, among the portrait painters whom she resembles. She is always in earnest about her women, and makes the reader in earnest too,—you cannot pass her characters by with mere amusement, as you can many of Shakespeare's and some of Scott's, and not a few of Miss Austen's. There is the Puritan intensity of feeling, the Miltonic weight of thought, in all George Eliot's drawings of women. If they are superficial in character and feeling, the superficiality is insisted on as a sort of crime. If they are not superficial, the depth is brought out with an energy that is sometimes almost painful. We have the same kind of exaltation of tone which Milton so dearly loved in most of George Eliot's poems; indeed, these poems have a distinctly Miltonic weight both of didactic feeling and of the rhythm which comes of it. In 'Armgart,' for example, there is all the Miltonic tone of feeling applied, in rhythm often almost as Miltonic, to measure the standard of a woman's ambition and devotion. Thus her world of women, at all events, is a world of larger stature than the average world we know; indeed, she can hardly sketch the shadows and phantoms by which so much of the real world is peopled, without impatience and scorn. She cannot laugh at the world—of women at least—as other writers equally great can. Where is there such a picture as Miss Austen's of Lydia Bennet in 'Pride and Prejudice,' or Mrs. Elton in 'Emma,' or even Emma herself, or Miss Crawford in 'Mansfield Park;' or even such pictures as Sir Walter Scott's Di Vernon and Catherine Seyton? With men, it is true, George Eliot can deal somewhat more lightly. . . . Our author probably indulges more neutrality of feeling in relation to men than she does in relation to women. She does not regard them as beings whose duty it is to be very much in earnest, and who are almost contemptible or wicked if they are otherwise. And yet she handles even men more gravely than most novelists. She has more of the stress and assiduity of Richardson than of the ease of Fielding in her drawing. Nevertheless, there are many of her male creations— Fred Vincy, in 'Middlemarch', is an excellent example—who have really but little earnestness in them, and yet who are not so consciously weighed in the balance and found wanting as the women in the same condition. There is something of the large and grave statuesque style in all George Eliot's studies of women. She cannot bear to treat them with indifference. If they are not what she approves, she makes it painfully, emphatically evident. If they are, she dwells upon their earnestness and aspirations with an almost Puritanic moral intensity, which shows how eagerly she muses on her ideal of women's life.   [R. H. HUTTON]

The Fortnightly Review, 1 November 1876

. . . In many things 'Daniel Deronda' is like the former novels of George Eliot, in some considerably unlike. It is written under the same urgent sense of the larger interests of mankind and of the duty each of us owes to all. To this view of life and conduct belongs a moral ardour which, rising to devotional pitch, utters its last aspiration in the cry—

> 'Oh may I join the choir invisible
> Whose music is the gladness of the world!'

Such is that religion of George Eliot's which, being 'something else than a private consolation,' many of the religious fail to under-

stand. Its influence governs all she writes. To exalt the social and
abase the selfish principle, to show the futility of merely personal
claims, cares, and cravings, to purify the passions by exhibiting
their fatal or miserable issues when they are centred in the individual alone—such are the moral purposes which we feel at work
beneath all her artistic purposes. Out of the resources of her genius,
this writer is accustomed to compose mottoes in various styles for
heading her own chapters. The following fragment in the style of
seventeenth-century prose is taken from a heading in 'Daniel
Deronda':—

'In all ages it hath been a favourite text that a potent love hath
the nature of an isolated fatality, whereto the mind's opinions and
wonted resolves are altogether alien. . . . Yet all love is not such,
even though potent, nay, this passion hath as large a scope as any
for allying itself with every operation of the soul; so that it shall
acknowledge an effect from the imagined flight of unknown firma-
ments, and have its scale set to the grander orbits of what has
been and shall be.'

In such a sentence on the nature of love we recognise at once
George Eliot's habitual drift. She will not say, with the old poets
and those who now-a-days share their temper, 'Love is enough.'
Pharamond, rather, must attend to his kingdom and forget
Azalaïs. Love must not lead the lover to break with duty or
renounce his past. Take warning by Tristram, Abailard, Romeo,
the old reckless heroes whose loves led only to disaster. To be
worthy of responsible modern souls—to lead to noble and harmonious issues—the love of man and woman must be brought into
conscious harmony with all the higher elements of their lives, and
identified, it may be, with some great social interest. The world is
not made for those who set private happiness in the first place; or
rather, the only true private happiness is to be found in the same
channels along which flow the currents of universal good.

In 'Daniel Deronda,' we feel ourselves more than ever encompassed with this sense of universal interests and outside forces. It
is brought home to us in one way when we are told to remember
that the days in which the actors of the story play their parts were
the days of the American war, 'when ideas were with fresh vigour
making armies of themselves, *and the universal kinship was declaring itself fiercely*; when women on the other side of the world would
not mourn for the husbands and sons who died bravely in a com-

mon cause, and men stinted of bread on our side of the world heard of that willing loss and were patient;' and in the same way, when elsewhere we are reminded how all this while events were making ready for the world-changing field of Sadowa. It is brought home to us in another way when the insignificance of the individual and his feelings among the mass is dwelt upon, as it is continually, and scorn is showered upon those who ignorantly cry out for happiness and expect the universe to be fashioned according to their desires. Some readers, indeed, are likely to feel that points of this kind are made too often, and, if they do not judge the American war and the German war irrelevant, at any rate to think some of the animadversions the author addresses to her own characters importunate. When any of these want their own way, and take it for granted things will turn out as they would like, they are not only chastened, but rebuked with bitterness. Of Gwendolen Harleth and her losses at play it is sarcastically said that '*the chances of roulette had not adjusted themselves to her claims;*' and in a hundred passages this reproof of 'claims' is the burden of the author's reflections. She speaks somewhere of the 'intolerance' which the experienced are prone to exhibit towards the outbreaks of 'the first rage of disappointment in life's morning'—'the passionate youthful rebellion against what is not fitly called pain, but rather the absence of joy.' And in the same breath she speaks of the '*self-enclosed unreasonableness and impiety*' of such feelings of disappointment and rebellion, and herself sets, I think, an example of the intolerance in question. She has no patience with those who expect good things without deserving them. She will by no means let people off when they are selfish, and takes the part of the species against the individual till we almost feel it is not fair, and want to go over to the other side. For after all there are two sides to these things; and if, in a fiction, love is too harshly sacrificed to duty, we incline to take love's part, and to say it is all very well, but there are cases where love must have his way before duty is possible; there is a certain measure of self-regard which is necessary to fruitful self-devotion; there are sacrifices which avail nothing, because they wither up in the victim all power of doing good to any one. If, again, a character is too sternly punished for expecting to find life pleasant, we are inclined to ask, but was it all his own, or her own, fault? are people taught when they are young what life is really like? and should not some of the chastisement fall upon mankind, upon the collective want of conscience which sends out poor human beings into the world under a delusion as to what the world has to offer them?

Every problem in conduct, every human action and situation, involves some issue or other between personal cravings and instincts and the laws that make for the common good. Most writers of fiction have looked at life, and described its actions and situations, from the point of view of the individual, and his feelings and experiences under trial; they have written in sympathy with their own characters in the struggle with the inexorable. George Eliot has changed the point of view; she has a sterner sense of the consequences and responsibilities of human action; she is severe upon her characters, and in sympathy, so to speak, with the inexorable. That a writer of fiction should have arisen who takes this new view of life's meaning, is a thing which marks an epoch; in finding room for these enlarged considerations, the art of fiction has taken a new departure. But the artist should be impartial, exhibiting all the phases of the conflict between desire and duty, what we would like and what we may have, but not taking a side too avowedly. By all means, let a work of imagination exhibit the career of a spoiled child, and purify our selfish passions by showing through what fires of probation the pampered one must go; but the lesson of the story will come out just as well, its imaginative effect will be just as clear and strong, if the moral is not too much proclaimed. A story-teller should beware—more even than other people—of loving mankind so well as to be unjust to particular men and women when they offend; and surely George Eliot is unjust, or at least needlessly sarcastic, with her own erring children; in the mingled mood of scorn and tenderness with which she handles their infirmities, scorn seems sometimes to predominate. . . .

. . . The art of fiction has reached its highest point in the hands of two women in our time. One of them has just been taken away, and as we read the work of the other who is left, it is natural that we should have hers also in our mind. Their excellences are in few things the same. The flow of George Eliot's writing, we have felt, is apt to be impeded with excess of thought, while of writing which does flow, and in flowing carry the reader delightfully along, George Sand is an incomparable mistress. But this is only the sign of deeper differences. George Sand excels in the poetical part of her art. George Eliot excels in the philosophical. Each is equally mistress of human nature and its secrets, but the one more by instinct, the other more by reflection. In everything which is

properly matter of the intellect, the English writer is the superior
of the French by far. She stands on different and firmer philosophical ground. George Sand had known and shared the two great
intellectual fevers of her time in France—the social fever of those
who hoped to end the unequal reign of wealth and privilege, and
by remodelled institutions to make human brotherhood a reality;
and the religious fever of those who, breaking with churches and
abandoning the incredible, yet sought an anchorage for the individual soul in communion with a deity above the definition of
dogma. Much of George Sand's work has in it the ferment of these
doctrines—socialism and theism—but without, perhaps, gaining
from the admixture. The quality of her speculative reflections is
not on a level with the quality of her creations; she imagines much
better than she thinks. On the other hand, it is not only that
George Eliot is of a different genius, and thinks at least as well as
she imagines; it is that she belongs to a school with which most
of us to-day are more in sympathy, and which, whether we hold
its principles final or not, at any rate stands on solid ground, and
tells us things fruitful in practice and luminous as far as they reach.
She is penetrated with the scientific spirit, and the conclusions of
the scientific spirit, in their most comprehensive, most ardent,
most generous shape, form the moral and intellectual foundation
of her art. Only, such is the nature of art, that when it too much
lays bare its own moral and intellectual foundations, it produces
less effect than when it conceals them. George Eliot, while she
speaks much more to our understanding, never speaks to our
imagination in so pure, single, and harmonious a way as George
Sand. I do not know that any one of the many and noble lessons
of George Eliot is brought home to us so perfectly as that one
which George Sand had at heart—the lesson that a woman must
begin her own emancipation by ceasing to hold herself a slave and
cheap; that she must become a free, responsible, individual human
being, recognising her own sacredness, being no more ready to
give herself in carelessness to the first asker than to sell herself in
infamy to the first bidder, but putting devotion to the proof,
judging before she chooses, living her own life, and valuing her
own soul. From romances so different as 'Mauprat' and 'Mademoi-
selle Merquem,' this one moral results in unescapeable evidence
and in a light that never fades from our mind. For George Sand
is so much of a poet and artist, that every touch of her work
helps instinctively to the effect, every image is conceived in

relation to the whole, nothing comes to jar or distract us. In the work of George Eliot, moral and philosophical problems do not clothe themselves, with the same certainty of instinct, in appropriate artistic forms. We have passages of first-rate art side by side with passages of philosophy; and sometimes the philosophy comes where we want the art, and gives us a character like Daniel Deronda himself, who seems constructed rather than created. . . .

SIDNEY COLVIN

The Westminster Review, July 1878

. . . One preliminary word. While we regard George Eliot as one of the greatest of story-tellers; as one of the greatest masters of the art of peopling the world of thought with veritable men and women; as a writer who transcends all writers of fiction in the richness of her pages in errant wisdom, in delicious humour and in the crowding thoughts and reflections which make her books an inexhaustible magazine of wayside philosophy, we confess at once to a much more deep and sincere admiration of George Eliot's earlier than of her later writings. While, in every book that bears her name, there is almost incomparable merit; in some of the most recent there are very grave faults. We cannot look with the like satisfaction on all her works. Our criticism cannot be one current of unmitigated praise; and therefore our task is not only difficult, but, in a sense, unpleasant. We could have wished to recognise a gradual growth of power, a gradual sublimation of purpose, a gradual increase of ease and mastery over the mere material of her art in every successive effort of her genius; but, to our thinking, the 'Scenes in Clerical Life,' are, in some ways, more admirable as complete works of simple art than the elaborately tedious efforts of her later years. Certainly, neither 'Middlemarch' nor 'Daniel Deronda' will, in their laborious length, or in their painful elaboration, compare with those effortless productions of her masterful genius which have taken a unique place in our literature under the titles of 'Silas Marner' and 'The Mill on the Floss.' There is the strength of growth about these—there is the weakness of planned effort about those. In these earlier works she moved with a grace and simplicity which can only be compared with Nature's motions—as in the wavy flight of a bird over a slipping river, or the unconscious ease of the sunflower as it follows the day with its own orb-like face. In the later works she moves with an artistic grace which is by no means despicable, but it is the grace as of society which has taken thought as to its courtesies, and is not averse to show the art of its smiles. True, these latter would have moved our most ready assent and most grateful admiration, had we not had her earlier works to judge her by. No one but herself could have lost reputation by two such works as 'Middlemarch' and 'Daniel Deronda.'. . .

The object of the novel writer is to tell a story. We do not say that his sole function is to amuse the idle, or to occupy empty hours. Too many people seem to think such the duty of the writer of fiction, but we would not degrade his high office and great duties by any such misapprehension. Still, the primary duty of such writers is to narrate, and where an author forgets that duty, and becomes speculative, expository, literary, or historical, to the neglect of the tale which has to be told, the result must necessarily be a failure. A story may carry instruction, it may have a moral, it may teach some truth of science, it may be a stimulus to action, a persuasion to well-doing, but when any one of these becomes the object of the tale, the work ceases to be a work of fictional art, and will probably be only second-rate as a treatise on ethics or on science, as an oration or a sermon. Now, any earnest human being may find it difficult in these days to remain indifferent to many paramount questions. Science none of us can ignore with impunity. Religious questions are rife, and dogmas are a 'drug in the market.' The age is full of questionings, and just because the answers are few, the intellectual activity is great, and the dissatisfaction which is the spring of all great achievements is common amongst us. It could not be expected that a woman like George Eliot could remain apart from the intense and rapid eddying currents of the life of the age. Even in her early life she entered into the religious questions by translating Strauss's 'Life of Christ,' and Feuerbach's 'Essence of Christianity,' and since that time much of the scientific life of the period has been reflected in her own life. She has lived intensely in relation to certain important problems, and these have influenced her, not only in her life, but in her art. It is here that we would have insisted upon separateness. All that is essentially human in George Eliot is compatible with a narrative which she may carry to the widest circle in space, and the most remote circle in time. Homer may be obsolete some day, but after two thousand years there are closenesses in his and our humanity which make his language ours, and George Eliot might expect to charm centuries

12

whose foundations are not yet laid, except in such books as her own. But as we said, to convey a tale one must make that the object, one must subordinate all one's own personal vanities, or affectations, or clevernesses, or eruditions, or sciences, and make the tale with the human beings whose doings and sufferings make the story all prominent. It is for this reason that the creation of human character is the primary merit of the novelist, for it is that which is the indispensable element of story-telling. But the inferior writers of fiction are always two-minded, they have a story to tell, and they have also to prove that they are excellent story-tellers, or that they know all science, or are 'well up' in art, or that they are anxious to save souls alive, and hence they fail. If they could have kept their pettiness apart from the tale, if they could have separated their vain or learned or religious selves from the narrative, they might have conveyed the incidents with explicable clearness, but they chose to be expository or what not, and they have been dull companions and disregarded teachers. The very intensity of their feelings about these matters has been their ruin. Their art was not all in all, their science or religion was something to them. So it has been with George Eliot to some extent. While she dissociated herself from to-day and the matters of the hour which had an intense personal interest for her, she was great. Her pictures of provincial life were exquisite. Other writers had chosen to dissociate their artistic from their personal interest by choosing the remote as a subject, and none have run the risk of bringing these into conflict by treating with scarcely concealed didacticism the great problems of the age. To Fielding and Austin and Scott these problems were as nothing compared with their art, and they have not risked that by the treatment of these. George Eliot has, and where she has made this endeavour, she has, as we think we have shown, failed. She has failed to subordinate her personal interests to the larger interests of her art; she has failed to see that there are questions of more importance to all ages than the science and the aspirations of this, and that her duty was to tell stories which would command the sympathies, not of the learned merely, but of the learned and simple; not of her own time only, but of all ages. . . .

The Quarterly Review, January 1879

'The Reflection of English Character in English Art'
. . . A rapid comparison between the method of the representative

novelists of our own time and those of the early part of the century, will show how materially social ideas of action have altered in the interval. Miss Austen in one class shall pair with George Eliot; in another Sir Walter Scott with Mr. Charles Reade. We take it that among novels describing social manners, 'Emma,' in point of construction, stands without a rival. The story relates the fortunes of a match-making heroine in a quiet country town. A more restricted subject or sphere cannot be imagined, yet so admirably are the involvements of the situation contrived, that the interest of the reader never flags. Many and various persons support the action; all of them present types of character with which we are familiar; but from the excellent humour, delicacy, and complete-ness with which they are drawn, they seem better representatives of the type than any we have observed ourselves. The dialogue is shrewd, natural, and well-bred. The whole of this well-proportioned story is comprised within four hundred pages. Contrast with it one of George Eliot's later novels, 'Daniel Deronda,' for instance. We say 'later novels,' for George Eliot's earlier works have a character of their own, which would render a comparison with Miss Austen quite inappropriate. There the former was on her own ground; she was writing about scenes and characters with which she had an instinctive sympathy; and her representations, in 'Adam Bede' and 'Silas Marner,' of the poetry and humour of English country life, have in their kind no equal. But in 'Middlemarch' and 'Daniel Deronda' she unconsciously provokes recollections of her predecessor, which are not altogether to the advantage of the taste of our own times. 'Daniel Deronda' deals with the same average good society as 'Emma,' a society whose principles, senti-ments, and manners, have been fixed by a more or less regular standard derived from the traditions of many generations. In the place, however, of the peaceful external atmosphere which must necessarily pervade an old society like this, the novel takes us into a world of mystery, philosophy, emotion, and crime. The story is rather ambitiously divided into eight books, each containing something like two hundred pages. It has two perfectly distinct plots, which scarcely anywhere touch each other, and never blend. The amount of action in each of these plots is infinitesimally small; the actors in the drama are commonplace. How, then, is the tale extended to such enormous length? By the analysis of conscious-ness. The reader is, so to speak, taken up by the author to a high mountain of metaphysics, from which he is bidden to look down on the petty drama beneath. At this elevation he sees, or is supposed to see, things in their true proportions; the place which the actors occupy in the order of the universe; the manner in which their actions are controlled by destiny; the *thoughts* that are passing in the minds of the suffering creatures exhibited to him. . . .

[W. J. COURTHOPE]

Blackwood's Magazine, February 1881

. . . It was well that a great genius arose to save for us pictures of a state of society that has now passed away. The Midlands in George Eliot's childhood still retained the quiet, old-fashioned, easy-going life of the last century. Railroads were unknown; newspapers had not reached the masses; politics commanded little general interest; the affairs of each small community were to itself all in all; and people cared little what went on in the next county, and still less what was happening in other countries. Such spirit of inquiry as was abroad found expression in religious dissent, which was then sufficiently uncommon to scandalise the well-to-do among the people, and sometimes to attract persecution, as in the case of poor Mr Tryan. If the people grumbled, it was at something that directly affected their own interests—such as tithes or taxes; and they cared little for the improvement of their political position. Squires were squires in those days, and rectors were rectors—great local magnates whose personal dispositions were everything to the people with whom they came in contact, and whose rights and privileges, however arbitrarily they might be exercised, were not to be called in question. Steam factories and machinery had not yet tended to extinguish individuality among the working classes, and a clever handicraftsman was a person of general consideration. The inn landlord and the parish clerk were people of social standing, and the mail-coachman a great public character. Education was confined to the few, and general knowledge was far from being either accurate or extensive. From the height of our own enlightenment, we are apt to look back with a species of contempt upon so primitive a state of society; and yet it was its quaintness and simplicity that fascinated George Eliot's mind and gave a colour to her genius. It is noteworthy that in 'Adam Bede' and in the 'Mill on the Floss,' where she is dealing with the older condition of the country, she is much more successful than in 'Felix Holt,' which belongs to the era of the Reform upheaval; and this would almost justify us in believing that she had seen less that was beautiful and lovable in the latter than in the former stage, though her sympathies were unmistakably with the newer epoch. The reality of her convictions never altogether gets the better of her sentimental liking for the England of her own early life; and she presents the singular case of one who is at once an advanced advocate of progress and an enthusiastic *laudator temporis acti*. 'Mine,' she playfully says, 'I fear, is not a well-regulated mind: it has an occasional tenderness for old abuses; it lingers with a certain fondness over the days of nasal clerks and top-booted parsons, and has a sigh for the departed shades of vulgar errors.' In the introduction of 'Felix Holt,' in the exquisite description of a stage-coach journey in the days before railways, the same key-note is struck. And who can forget the beautiful lament over the death of 'Fine Old Leisure,' who 'read only one newspaper, innocent of leaders, and was free from that periodicity of sensations which we call post-time? He was a contemplative, rather stout gentleman, of excellent digestion—of quiet perceptions, undiseased by hypothesis: happy in his inability to know the causes of things, preferring the things themselves.' There was much quiet humour and sometimes a good deal of easy banter mixed in her records of old country recollections; but we cannot mistake the kindly and genial associations which in her after-life were mingled with the retrospect of the society in which her youth was passed. . . .

[Written by Alexander Allardyce, and revised by William Blackwood, Mr. Langford and Sir Edward Hamley]

The Contemporary Review, January 1881

. . . She sympathizes with the love of man to man, we should say, in proportion as it is unlike the love of man to God. There was much in her writings—there must be much in the utterance of all lofty and imaginative spirits—which tells against this description. In the relation of the human spirit to the Father of spirits lies hid the germ of every human relation; there is none which does not, dimly and feebly, foreshadow that which lies at the root of all. And least inadequately, least vaguely is this foreshadowed in that love which gathers up the whole being—that love which, while it is felt in some sense by the whole animal creation, is yet that which, in its highest form, most opens to man the true meaning of a spiritual world. The love of man to woman, and woman to man, is the one profound and agitating emotion which is known to ordinary human hearts, and its portraiture, therefore, attempted by a thousand ineffectual chroniclers, is the most trite and commonplace of all themes of fiction. But when a writer arises who can hold up a mirror to this part of our being, he or she opens to us something of the infinite; for the most shallow and *borné* nature, so far as it has partaken in this great human experience, has a window whence it may gaze towards all that is eternal. And it must always seem false to speak of one who has the power of recalling an emotion in which man is lifted above and beyond the limits of his individual being as wanting in sympathy with that impulse which lifts him above those limits most completely. This reservation we would make most fully, but the very gradation of interest in George Eliot's painting of human love seems to us explained and completed by that vacuum which it surrounds. There is no grade of this emotion that she has not touched more or less slightly—the strange stirrings of heart at a first glimpse of the goal; the wondrous sudden flooding of life with joy that comes of its certainty; the quiet conjugal repose of two hearts that have added long familiarity to the first vivid love without dimming it; the irresistible rush of a guilty passion and the strange delights that are hidden in its horror—all these she has so painted that her imagination has interpreted to many a loving heart its own experience. But we think most of her readers will agree with us in the conclusion that, with few exceptions, human love is interesting in her pages in inverse proportion as it bears the impress of what is divine. We linger over the relation between a heartless and shallow girl and an enthusiastic student of science whose life she spoils, with absorbing interest, and we yawn over the courtship of a shadowy hero and heroine who seem each to have been intended as a type of all that is worthy of reverence. We are riveted by the description of a wife's anguish as she recognizes the false heart behind the fair face, or the cold heart behind the seeming profundity of thought, but we find the love of the graceful maiden for the virtuous Radical not greatly above the level of ordinary circulating library interest. Almost always where love looks *downwards*, whether for good or for evil, her power is at its highest. Where it looks upwards, with few exceptions, her power seems to ebb, and sometimes (so we at least feel in the love of Deronda and Myra) altogether to depart. With few exceptions we have said, we mean in fact with one exception, but that is certainly a significant one. If there is an emotion which brings the heart into close neighbourhood with that region where man finds intercourse with God, it is that which unites man and woman by a love that lacks nothing of passion but its exclusiveness. This love is a commoner thing than is supposed, but its delineation is rarer, we believe, than itself, and two passages in George Eliot's novels contain more adequate suggestion of what some have found the most elevating of human communion than we know in the whole of fiction besides. One of these is the description of the last conversation between Gwendoline and Deronda, the other is the intercourse between the broken-hearted heroine and the consumptive clergyman, in 'Janet's Repentance.' Still on the whole we may say (and even these pictures are not altogether exceptions to the rule) that something of mistake mixes in most upward-looking devotion as George Eliot paints it. That devotion of which all such is a feeble prophecy and type, must therefore take the very centre and focus of error.

Must one who feels this severance of love of man from faith in God, the great misfortune of our time, yet allow that the thing that is left acquires, for the moment, a sudden influx of new energy by the very fact of its severance? It would not be looking facts fairly in the face to deny that the genius of George Eliot seems to show such a result. Nor is there any real difficulty in making the concession. A bud may open more quickly in water in a warm room than on its parent stem, although thus the seed will never ripen. We may transfer conviction to a more genial atmosphere at the very moment we sever it from its root, and we must wait long to discover that the life that is quickened in it is also threatened. . . .

The Atlantic Monthly, May 1885

'George Eliot's Life'

. . . It is striking that from the first her conception of the novelist's task is never in the least as the game of art. The most interesting passage in Mr. Cross's volumes is, to my sense, a simple sentence in a short entry in her journal in the year 1859, just after she had finished the first volume of The Mill on the Floss (the original title of which, by the way, had been Sister Maggie): 'We have just finished reading aloud Père Goriot, a hateful book.' That Balzac's masterpiece should have elicited from her only this remark, at a time, too, when her mind might have been opened to it by her own activity of composition, is significant of so many things that the few words are, in the whole Life, those I should have been most sorry to lose. Of course they are not all George Eliot would have had to say about Balzac, if some other occasion than a simple jotting in a diary had presented itself. Still, what even a jotting may *not* have said after a first perusal of Le Père Goriot is eloquent; it illuminates the author's general attitude with regard to the novel, which, for her, was not primarily a picture of life, capable of deriving a high value from its form, but a moralized fable, the last word of a philosophy endeavoring to teach by example.

This is a very noble and defensible view, and one must speak respectfully of any theory of work which would produce such fruit as Romola and Middlemarch. But it testifies to that side of George Eliot's nature which was weakest—the absence of free aesthetic life (I venture this remark in the face of a passage quoted from one of her letters in Mr. Cross's third volume); it gives the hand, as it were, to several other instances that may be found in the same pages. 'My function is that of the *aesthetic*, not the doctrinal teacher; the rousing of the nobler emotions, which make mankind desire the social right, not the prescribing of special measures, concerning which the artistic mind, however strongly moved by social sympathy, is often not the best judge.' That is the passage referred to in my parenthetic allusion, and it is a good general description of the manner in which George Eliot may be said to have acted on her generation; but the 'artistic mind,' the possession of which it implies, existed in her with limitations remarkable in a writer whose imagination was so rich. We feel in her, always, that she proceeds from the abstract to the concrete; that her figures and situations are evolved, as the phrase is, from her moral conscious-ness, and are only indirectly the products of observations. They are deeply studied and elaborately justified, but they are not *seen* in the irresponsible plastic way. The world was, first and foremost, for George Eliot, the moral, the intellectual world; the personal spectacle came after; and lovingly, humanly, as she regarded it, we constantly feel that she cares for the things she finds in it only so far as they are types. The philosophic door is always open, on her stage, and we are aware that the somewhat cooling draught of ethical purpose draws across it. This constitutes half the beauty of her work; the constant reference to ideas may be an excellent source of one kind of reality—for, after all, the secret of seeing a thing well is not necessarily that you see nothing else. Her pre-occupation with the universe helped to make her characters strike you as also belonging to it; it raised the roof, widened the area, of her aesthetic structure. Nothing is finer, in her genius, than the combination of her love of general truth and love of the special case; without this, indeed, we should not have heard of her as a novelist, for the passion of the special case is surely the basis of the storyteller's art. All the same, that little sign of all that Balzac failed to suggest to her showed at what perils the special case got itself considered. . . .

The truth is, perception and reflection, at the outset, divided George Eliot's great talent between them; but, as time went on, circumstances led the latter to develop itself at the expense of the former—one of these circumstances being apparently the influence of George Henry Lewes. Lewes was interested in science, in cosmic problems; and though his companion, thanks to the original bent of her versatile, powerful mind, needed no impulse from without to turn herself to speculation, yet the contagion of his studies pushed her further than she would otherwise have gone in the direction of *scientific* observation, which is but another form of what I have called reflection. Her early novels are full of natural as distinguished from systematic observation, though even in them it is less the dominant will, I think, than the love of the 'moral,' the reaction of thought in the face of the human comedy. They had observation sufficient, at any rate, to make their fortune, and it may well be said that that is enough for any novel. In Silas Marner, in Adam Bede, the quality seems gilded by a sort of autumn haze, an afternoon light, of meditation, which mitigates the sharpness of portraiture. I doubt very much whether the author herself had a clear vision, for instance, of the marriage of Dinah Morris to Adam, or of the rescue of Hetty from the scaffold at the eleventh hour. The reason of this may be, indeed, that her perception was a perception of nature much more than of art, and that these particular incidents do not belong to nature (to my sense, at least); by which I do not mean that they belong to a very happy art. I cite them, on the contrary, as an evidence of artistic weakness; they are a very good example of the view in which a story must have marriages and rescues in the nick of time as a matter of course. I must add, in fairness to George Eliot, that the marriage of the nun-like Dinah, which shocks the reader, who sees in it a base concession, was a *trouvaille* of Lewes's, and is a small sign of that same faulty judgment in literary things which led him to throw his influence on the side of her writing verse—verse which is *all* reflection, with direct, vivifying vision remarkably absent.

It is a part of this same limitation of the pleasure she was capable of taking in the fact of representation for itself that the various journals and notes of her visits to the Continent are, though by no means destitute of the tempered enjoyment of foreign sights, which was as near as she ever came to rapture, singularly vague in expression on the subject of the general and particular spectacle—the life and manners, the works of art. She enumerates diligently all the pictures and statues she sees, and the way she does so is a proof of her active, earnest intellectual habits; but it is rarely apparent that they have, as the phrase is, said much to her, or that what they have said is one of their deeper secrets. She is capable of writing, after coming out of the great chapel of San Lorenzo, in Florence, that 'the world-famous statues of Michael Angelo on the tombs . . . remained to us as affected and exaggerated in the original as in copies and casts.' That sentence startles one, on the part of the author of Romola, and that Mr. Cross should have printed it is a commendable proof of his impartiality. . . .

HENRY JAMES

Notes on the Reviewers

ALLARDYCE, ALEXANDER (Obituary Notice on George Eliot, *Blackwood's Magazine*, February 1881). Assistant editor to William Blackwood, and employee of the firm. Previously edited newspapers in India and Ceylon, and worked for *The Spectator*.

BLACKWOOD, JOHN (Letters to George Eliot). 1818–79. Fourth son of William Blackwood, the founder of the firm. Managed the firm's London branch until 1845, then returned to Edinburgh to edit *Blackwood's Edinburgh Magazine* (usually known as 'Maga'): it was because Lewes had often contributed to Maga that the manuscript of George Eliot's first book was sent to Blackwood's. After his brother's death in 1852, John Blackwood took most of the responsibility for book publishing as well. There is a large and interesting correspondence extant between him and George Eliot, and the letters printed above are only samples. His nephew Willie (son of his elder brother Major William Blackwood, d 1861) succeeded him in the firm, and had begun to do so while George Eliot was still alive: Willie helped to revise Allardyce's obituary notice.

BROOME, SIR FREDERICK NAPIER (*Middlemarch*, *The Times*, 7 March 1873). 1842–96. Colonial Governor. Sheep-farmer in New Zealand, 1857–69; Colonial Secretary of Natal 1875, of Mauritius 1880; Governor of Australia 1882–90, of Barbados 1890. Published some poetry, and was a frequent contributor to *The Times*.

COLLINS, REV. W. LUCAS (*Middlemarch*, *Blackwood's Magazine*, December 1872). 1817–87. Editor of 'Ancient Classics for English Readers', in which he wrote the volumes on *The Iliad*, *The Odyssey*, Aristophanes, Lucian, Vergil, Plautus, Terence, Cicero, Livy and Thucydides; and a number of miscellaneous works of literary criticism.

COLVIN, SIR SIDNEY (*Middlemarch*, *Fortnightly Review*, 19 January 1873; *Daniel Deronda* (extract in General section), *Fortnightly Review*, 1 November 1876). 1845–1927. Well-known critic of art and literature. Slade Professor of Fine Art at Cambridge 1873–85; Director of the Fitzwilliam Museum 1876; Keeper of Prints in the British Museum 1883–1912. Wrote the 'English Men of Letters' volumes on Landor and Keats, and several other critical works, of which the most celebrated was *John Keats: his Life and Poetry*, 1917. His *Memories and Notes*, 1921, has something on George Eliot. Colvin was a friend of Robert Louis Stevenson's, and edited his letters.

COURTHOPE, W. J. ('The Reflection of English Character in English Art', *Quarterly Review*, January 1879). 1842–1917. Civil servant and scholar; Professor of Poetry at Oxford 1895–1900. Edited the works of Pope, in ten volumes, with Whitwell Elwin; and wrote a valuable *History of English Poetry* (1895–1910). Also published a few volumes of his own verse.

DALLAS, E. S. (*Adam Bede, The Mill on the Floss, Felix Holt*; in *The Times*, 12 April 1859, 19 May 1860, 26 June 1866). 1828–79. Critic and regular reviewer for *The Times*. Published *Poetics, an Essay in Poetry*, 1852, and *The Gay Science*, 1866. Dallas was a pioneer in the use of psychological ideas for literary criticism, and some of his writing has a surprisingly modern ring. This interest can be seen in his remarks on 'the region of latent thoughts, and unconscious or but semi-conscious feelings' in his review of *Adam Bede*.

DOWDEN, EDWARD ('George Eliot', *Contemporary Review*, August 1872). 1843–1913. Professor of English Literature at Trinity College, Dublin, from 1867 to his death. Wrote many works of literary criticism. *Shakespeare, his Mind and Art*, 1875, was followed by editions of many of Shakespeare's plays. Published a volume of poems in 1876: *Studies in Literature*, 1878; *Life of Shelley*, 1886; *Transcripts and Studies*, 1888; *New Studies in Literature*, 1895; *Essays Modern and Elizabethan*, 1910; and biographies of Southey, Browning and Montaigne.

HUTTON, R. H. (*Daniel Deronda*—various notices in *The Spectator* during 1876; and probably also *Romola* and *Middlemarch* in the same paper, 18 July 1863 and 1 June 1872). 1826–97. Joint editor of *The Spectator*. Began life as a Unitarian, and intended to enter the ministry; after abandoning this intention he edited *The*

Inquirer (the Unitarian weekly) 1851–3, but his views were unacceptable to its readers. He later became an Anglican, with High Church, even Roman Catholic sympathies. In 1861 Meredith Townsend, who had just bought *The Spectator*, invited Hutton to join him as co-editor, with responsibility for the literary section, a post he held until his death. He always remained interested in theology, on which he wrote regularly. Published *Essays Theological and Literary*, 1871, and several other works. Friend of Bagehot, F. D. Maurice and Gladstone.

JACOBS, JOSEPH ('Mordecai: A Protest against the Critics' in *MacMillan's Magazine*, June 1877). 1854–1916. Literary scholar and writer on Jewish subjects. Edited a number of English classics, as well as the Jewish yearbooks and wrote several books on Jewish thought and history. This essay was republished in his *Jewish Ideas and other Essays* 1896, with a few interesting remarks on George Eliot in the Introduction. 'George Eliot's novels were regarded by us not so much as novels, but rather as applications of Darwinism to life and art. . . . Nowadays, when their *Tendenz* is discredited, their artistic qualities have been depreciated far below their just value.' He spoke of the importance of *Daniel Deronda* in his own intellectual development, stimulating an awareness of the historic aspects of Judaism. 'Spinoza envisaged for me the Jewish ideals in their static form, George Eliot transferred my attention to them in their dynamic development.'

JAMES, HENRY (1843–1916) is of course the novelist. He wrote several essays on George Eliot; here for convenient reference, is a list of principal ones: 1 'Felix Holt the Radical' in *The Nation*, 16 August 1866, reprinted in *Notes and Reviews*, 1921 (extract on p. 72); 2 'The Novels of George Eliot' in *The Atlantic Monthly*, October 1866, reprinted in *Views and Reviews* 1908 (extract on p. 42); 3 'Middlemarch' in *Galaxy*, March 1873, reprinted posthumously in *The House of Fiction* 1957; 4 '*Daniel Deronda*: a Conversation' in *The Atlantic Monthly*, December 1876, reprinted in *Partial Portraits*, 1888 (see p. 148). After her death he reviewed Cross's *Life* in *The Atlantic Monthly*, May 1885, reprinted in *Partial Portraits*, 1888.

JEWSBURY, GERALDINE (*Adam Bede*, *The Athenaeum*, 26

February 1859) 1812–80. Novelist, friend and correspondent of Jane Welsh Carlyle. Published *The Half Sisters*, 1845, *Constance Herbert*, 1855, and other novels. *Constance Herbert* was reviewed by George Eliot, and accused (though she treated the book with respect) of 'copy-book morality': 'the notion that duty looks stern, but all the while has her hand full of sugar-plums, with which she will reward us by-and-by ... undermines all true moral development.'

LAWRENNY, H. (*Middlemarch*, *The Academy*, 1 January 1873). Unknown. Kenneth Graham, in his useful study *English Criticism of the Novel 1865–1900*, identifies this reviewer as Edith Simcox also virtually unknown, but the author of three books: *Episodes in the Lives of Men, Women and Lovers*; *Natural Law, an Essay in Ethics*; and *Primitive Civilisations*.

LUCAS, SAMUEL (*Scenes of Clerical Life*, *The Times*, 2 January 1858). 1811–65. Regular reviewer for *The Times* during the last ten years of his life. Quaker, and supporter of various liberal and radical causes. Member of the Anti-Corn Law League; helped to found the Lancashire (afterwards National) Public Schools Association, and wrote a good deal on education; an energetic member of the Society for Repeal of Taxes on Knowledge. Edited the *Morning Star*, organ of the Manchester Liberals. Supported the North in the American Civil War.

ROBERTSON, REV. J. C. (*Adam Bede*, *Quarterly Review*, October 1860). 1813–82. Church historian. Canon of Canterbury, and Professor of Ecclesiastical History at King's College, London 1864–74. His major work was a *History of the Christian Church*, 4 vols, 1852–73. Friend of William MacPherson, editor of the *Quarterly*, and a frequent contributor to it.

SAINTSBURY, GEORGE (*Daniel Deronda*, *The Academy*, 9 September 1876). 1845–1933. Professor of Rhetoric and English Literature at Edinburgh, 1895–1915, and one of the best known literary historians of his time. His writings covered a huge range (he wrote Histories of both English and French literature): as a critic he was enthusiastic, systematic and—by any modern standards—naive. But the youthful notice reprinted here shows him in a surprisingly acute and lively vein.